I GO to the
ROCK

I GO to the ROCK

Copyright © 2014 by Ruthie Jacobsen

Authors:
> Ruthie Jacobsen
> Dwight K. Nelson
> Fredrick A. Russell

Editor: Don Jacobsen

Cover and interior design, Diane Baier

Cover photograph, © Meinzahn, istockphoto.com

Published by HighWalk Productions, Inc.
PO Box 26, Hiawassee, GA 30546

ISBN: 978-0-615-77964-5

CONTENTS

I GO TO THE ROCK …
AND I DISCOVER:

- There is no Rock like our God. I Sam. 2:2
- They drank from the spiritual Rock that followed them, and that Rock was Christ. I Cor. 10:4
- My God is my Rock in whom I take refuge. II Sam. 23:3
- Be my Rock of refuge … for you are my Rock and my fortress. Ps 71:3
- He alone is my Rock and my salvation. Ps. 62:2
- Who is the Rock except our God? II Sam. 22:32
- Do not tremble, do not be afraid … there is no other Rock. Isa. 4:8
- Exalted be God, the Rock, my Savior! II Sam 22:47
- Trust in the Lord forever, for the Lord, the Lord, is the Rock eternal. Isa 26:4
- To you I call, O Lord, my Rock … hear my cry for mercy. Ps 28:1, 2
- You are my Father, my God, the Rock, my Savior. Ps 89:26
- Lead me to the Rock that is higher than I. Ps 61:2
- The Lord is my Rock, my fortress and deliverer. Ps 18:2
- He is the Rock … a faithful God who does no wrong. Deut 32:4
- O Lord, my Rock, and my Redeemer. Ps 19:14
- The Lord Lives! Praise be to my Rock! Ps 18:46
- Come, let us sing for joy to the Lord, let us shout aloud to the Rock of our salvation. Ps 95:1

INTRODUCTION

More than twenty times Scripture refers to God as a steady Rock for His people. The symbol is an apt one. Rock is stable; our God is unchanging. Rock is durable; our God endures forever. We set our buildings on rock; our God is the sure foundation. A rock can cast a shadow; our God is a Shadow in a weary land. A rock can survive a storm; our God is a refuge. Rock is everywhere; our God is omnipresent. The similes would make a long list.

Dottie Rambo picked up the strength of the imagery when she wrote:

> Where do I go when there's no one else to turn to?
> Who do I talk to when no one wants to listen?
> Who do I lean on when there's no foundation stable?
> I go to the Rock, I know He's able, I go to the Rock.
>
> Where do I hide till the storms have all passed over?
> Who do I run to when the winds of sorrow threaten?
> Is there a refuge in the time of tribulation?
> When my soul needs consolation, I go to the Rock.
>
> I go to the Rock for my salvation.
> I go to the Stone that the builders rejected.
> I run to the Mountain and the Mountain stands by me.
> When the earth all around me is sinking sand,
> On Christ the solid Rock I stand.
> When I need a shelter, when I need a friend, I go to the
> Rock.

This is a unique book. Three Spirit-filled preachers— Ruthie Jacobsen, Dwight Nelson, and Fredrick Russell—have contributed compelling insights into their own journey to the

Rock. Their messages are biblical, personal, and passionate. They are authentic, vulnerable, and motivating.

You'll like the fact that the messages first saw the light of day as sermons preached to live congregations; for that reason they tend to carry the informality and brisk pace of the spoken word. We think you'll find the book a joyous read and valuable in your journey, too.

Chapter 1

God's Set Time

Fredrick K. Russell

I'm not going to try to define "breakthrough prayer." I'm going to let God define it as we see Him doing what He does best. But let me define what prayer is. This is incredible: Prayer is the opening of the heart so we can receive all the good things that God has for us every single day. It's like sitting down at a table that God has prepared for us and He says, "I have everything you need for today. All the grace. All the wisdom. All the provisions that you need, but sit down at the table and eat. Don't be so rushed, so busy that you try to live without My supply."

And prayer is simply that, we come and we sit at God's table. The problem is that a lot of us go rushing off before we sit and receive. When answers don't come on our schedule we are inclined to get impatient. But I want you to know that God has a set time in which He answers prayer. It's not our time; it's His time, His set time. In His wisdom He will not allow us either to rush or to delay His set time.

Let me ask you a question: Have you ever—or maybe you are you now—praying for something and you pray and you pray what you thought was a long time and God still did not come through? I suspect that all of us could tell stories about that.

Are you praying for something right now and you're waiting for God to answer?

You pray and you wait and you pray and you wait, and you start to wonder if God is listening. Let me show you something remarkable; it's called the set time.

In Genesis Chapter 15, Abraham is praying for a son. At

this point in the story he has been praying this same prayer, placing his situation before God, not for six months, not for a year, but for ten long years.

Have you ever prayed for something for ten years? Abraham begins his prayer that he might have a son in Genesis 12 and by the time we reach Genesis 15, he has been praying for ten years. I have prayed for some things three weeks and I was already impatient with God.

In Genesis 15, Abraham is talking to God and God is also talking back to him, because prayer in its essence is not only when I'm talking to God but is also a time when God talks back to me. And let me give you a little secret: The more time we spend with God, the more often we are able to detect the sound of His voice.

When I first met my wife, Brenda, it was at the old South Atlantic Conference campground kitchen in Orangeburg, SC. She was standing in line waiting to get her lunch. I remember it well! We talked for just a few minutes and then we both went our separate ways. Now suppose I had called her on the phone the next day. I would not have recognized her voice and she would not have recognized mine. But today, thirty years later, Brenda can call me anytime, morning, noon, or night, and she doesn't have to say "Freddie, this is Brenda." When she opens her mouth, I know it's my wife because I've spent a lot of time with her. I know what her voice sounds like and I've learned that the more time I spend with God, the more I can detect His voice when He speaks.

So Abraham is in dialogue with God and in Genesis 15:1, it says, "After this the Word of the Lord came to Abraham in a vision, 'Don't be afraid Abraham. I am your Shield, I am your Great Reward.'"

Remember that Abraham has been longing for God to answer a prayer for ten straight years, so Abraham says in verse 2, "Sovereign Lord, what can you give me (as a 'very great reward') since I have remained childless and the one who would inherit my estate is my servant. ... ?" Abraham is saying, "God, You are offering me a great reward but You haven't even answered the simple prayer I've been praying to You for ten years. You want me to be the father of a nation, but You've left me childless."

Now follow the dialogue here: "Then the Word of the Lord came to Abraham: 'This man (his servant) will not be your heir but a son who is your own flesh and blood will be your heir.'" He (God) took Abraham outside and said, 'Look up at the sky and count the stars, if indeed you can count them.'" Then He promises, "So shall your offspring be."

Now I don't know about you but I might be saying something like this: "God, I don't have any children … none … and you are saying that my heirs will be as the stars of the sky. That's not a good illustration, God, because I'm not looking for all of those, I just want one."

Now, remember, Abraham has been praying this same prayer for ten long years.

When we get to Chapter 16 of Genesis we discover an interesting detail. Abraham and Sarah are getting old. When you're approaching eighty-five or ninety years of age you are biologically challenged when it comes to having children. At that point, Sarah is getting old and she knows. She no longer has to look at the clock; the clock itself has stopped.

When you see the months—or years—passing and God is not answering the prayer, the first temptation is often to try and answer it yourself. I talk to people all the time who get themselves into situations because they jump ahead of God and attempt to answer their prayer on their own. By the way, when you answer the prayer, it still isn't really answered and you often end up with more questions than answers.

So Sarah has this brilliant idea. She says, "Hold it here, *I'm* getting old, and *he's* getting old, but I have this great plan." She reasons, "I've got this 18-year-old servant girl named Hagar. Suppose Abraham were to sleep with her and she gets pregnant and has a baby. Because Hagar is my servant girl, the baby will be mine."

So she says to herself, "I'm going to talk to Abraham about this but I know Abraham is going to say 'No!' He's going to say that we are not crossing that line. We're not going there." But she gets up her nerve and says to Abraham, "Husband, you know, I've been thinking about this whole situation and about us not having a child, and I've got an idea."

Abraham is still listening so she goes on, "Well I've got this 18-year-old servant girl and I was thinking that if you slept with her and then we had a baby by her it would be our baby." Incredibly, Abraham agrees.

He sleeps with Hagar. Hagar does get pregnant and Ishmael is born. But, predictably, it doesn't work out well for the family. In fact, Hagar soon develops a taunting attitude toward Sarah and it's finally decided that the house isn't big enough for both women so Abraham is forced to send Hagar and her baby into the wilderness alone.

Now let me focus the situation for you. Abraham and Sarah took things in their own hands and when you answer your own prayers, you don't get God's solution. Abraham and Sarah didn't solve the problem, they ended up complicating it. God wanted to give them Isaac, the son of promise, but they were willing to settle for Ishmael. They were not willing to wait for God's set time.

You may have been willing to settle for an Ishmael when God wanted to give you Isaac. You can sense that God said, "If you had waited, I would have given you an Isaac blessing but you ran ahead, you settled for an Ishmael blessing. You married that person anyhow. You wanted to take that job and I told you to wait. Here's the one I wanted for you." What I'm telling you is, when you call out to God and you ask Him and it seems like a delay, don't dash ahead; you are only complicating life and settling for less than God's best.

In Chapter 18 a fascinating narrative develops; Abraham receives three visitors to his tent encampment in the desert. At this time Abraham is nearly a hundred years old, actually ninety-nine. Remember he began to pray the prayer when he was seventy-five. Now twenty-four years have passed. And when twenty-four years have passed, many of us would be ready to say, "Maybe, just maybe, God is not going to answer this one."

So Abraham is standing outside of his tent there in the desert and these three strangers appear. Because he has the gift of hospitality Abraham invites them to stay for a meal. As they eat he begins to have a conversation, but he quickly discovers there is something unique about these three men.

In v. 9 one of them asks, "Where is your wife, Sarah?" "Over there in the tent," Abraham replies. One of them responds, "I will surely return to you about this time next year and Sarah your wife will have a son." Now, you and I might have been tempted to say, "Here we go again ... I wish I could believe you, but we've been down that road already ... for nearly a quarter of a century."

And Sarah, the Bible says, listening at the entrance to her tent, was past—way past—the age of child bearing. So Sarah laughed to herself. She muses, "This isn't going to happen; I'm 'worn out' and my husband is too old." I love the Lord's heart-stopping response. It's in v. 14 ... memorize the verse if you haven't already. Here it is: "Is anything too hard for the Lord?" I want you to see that how we answer that question determines both the strength and the joy of our journey.

You may have been praying for children for a long time and you think it will never happen. You may have been asking God for a husband or wife. You may have been pleading for help in your career. For the conversion of a spouse. You may need an intervention in a stormy relationship, and all the evidence suggests that God isn't listening. But remember the response from God. "Is anything too hard for the Lord?" In His time, at the set time, "All things are possible with God." All things. Big truth here: You're not waiting, then, for God's answer; you're waiting for God's time.

We pick up the story in Genesis 21. It's a year later. "Now the Lord was gracious to Sarah as He had said, and the Lord did for Sarah what He had promised. Sarah became pregnant and bore a son to Abraham in his old age, *at the very time* God had promised him." At the set time. On time. On God's time. Hallelujah! The God we serve is never late.

Not long ago my wife, Brenda, found a lump on her

collar bone. She didn't know what it was so she finally went to the doctor. He examined her and then said, "Mrs. Russell, this doesn't look good at all; we need to schedule a biopsy."

She went in for the biopsy, and the doctor gets this look on his face and he says, "I'll call you in a couple of days." I remember the morning he called. Brenda and I waited for the phone to ring. We were praying that what the doctor was inferring would not be.

The phone call came at eleven something that morning. Brenda was very calm—a lot calmer than I was. She picked up the phone and I heard her say, "Yes doctor, yes doctor. Oh! My God. Yes doctor. I'll be in."

She hung the phone up but I'm waiting, "Okay Brenda what is it?" She said, "The doctor says that I have cancer." The only thing I remember is falling off my bed in the bedroom and being curled up on the floor in a fetal position.

I couldn't cry, all I can do was wail. "Oh, God!" I wailed and I wailed and I wailed and I kept saying, "God why? I'm serving Your people, God. I'm doing the best I can, God, I'm giving my all, and now look … my wife has been diagnosed with Hodgkin's lymphoma." So we began to pray, "God, You've got to come through for us here. Father don't let this go any further. God, stop this disease. Stop it, God. Please, Father, I'm calling on You for help. Please!"

I went downstairs to my office. "Please God! Please!" I shouted at Him.

They scheduled her for chemo treatments, a regimen of twelve. So we began to call all the Adventist lifestyle centers around the country asking them, "Please, is there any way you could help her without going through this chemo?" They responded, "Mrs. Russell we cannot help you; all we can tell you is to go through the chemo, then come to us and we will rebuild your immune system through some natural means." We just kept praying, "God help us."

I remember that first chemo treatment because some had told us, "Surely, Pastor Freddy, God is going to come through for you." And I prayed, "It's me calling, God, it's Freddy. You are going to come through, right?"

At the first chemo treatment, I remember when they put the port in and the chemicals began to flow into her body. My wife is not that big and several hours later into the evening she got sick—really sick. She was throwing up and just feeling terrible. She couldn't do anything for two or three days. It was worse than I had thought it would be; she had no weight to lose, and I was in anguish, feeling totally helpless. I said, "God, look at my wife. God, if you don't come through this woman is going to die. She cannot take this."

We went to the second treatment and she got weaker. I remember after about the third treatment I was sitting in the bathroom with her … she was crying, combing her hair and the hair was coming out in clumps. "Oh my God. Oh my God, You've got to help us here," was all I could pray. The weeks were going by and she was weakening and becoming more and more frail. Her hair was going and I said "God, this is not going to last much longer unless You come through. Father … we need Your healing touch here. God, we know You can do this. You've got to come through." And I'm crying out loud to God. I'm saying, "God I didn't know it could get this bad. … " I said "Lord, You know I'm trying to trust You here. Father, she is going quick. Father, please. Help us!"

God allowed that thing to go month after month after month. No answers, no voice from the heavens. Nothing. I remember the Sabbath morning she came down the stairs and said, "Freddie I can't do this anymore. I cannot take any more chemo. Dying can't be worse than this."

Then God miraculously led us to find this little Lifestyle Center that was willing to accept her. She went there and they began to build up her immune system and her strength started to return. I remember the day she came home and I picked her up at Dulles Airport outside of DC. She looked beautiful to me as she came out of the terminal. She looked a little healthier though she was still thin. But she had this look in her eyes that said, "God is going to restore me to health; I am going to be okay!"

We kept praying. We kept praying and some months later

she went back to the doctor. He examined her carefully, then looked into her face and said, "Mrs. Russell we cannot find any trace of cancer in your body."

Through all those months of waiting, we didn't know. We didn't. But God says, "Freddie, Brenda, I've got a set time for you. I'm not going to heal things overnight. Sometimes I do, but this one we're going to let run its course. But you can know I'm going to heal her." God was saying, "When you started praying to me the first time, I already had the set time; there was never any doubt when I was going to do this."

I don't know what you're praying for today, but this I do know. God is on your side, and in His time and in His way He will meet your every need and more. His invitation is, "Come to the table, sit down. Don't be in such a rush. Let's talk about what you need. Talk to me. I will answer in My set time."

We seek His presence, not His miracles. When He comes He brings His miracles with Him. Do you know this song?

This is the air I breathe,
Your holy presence
Living in me.
This is my daily bread
Your very Word
Spoken through the years
And I'm desperate for you.
And I'm lost without you.

This we know: Even when we cannot feel His hand we can still trust His heart.

CHAPTER 2

HEARING VOICES

Dwight K. Nelson

It all began when I started hearing voices. For three weeks in a row I really was hearing voices. Not the kind of voices that frighten you, but those that get your attention. Voices from unexpected people, serendipitous moments, unexpected encounters. One of the voices, though, I knew to be the voice of God. Let me explain.

On a campus like the one where I work, the world runs at full throttle. Life is managed by calendars and class schedules. And bells—always bells. No sooner is one deadline passed than we plunge headlong into the next. Read, write, research, dig, back to the lab, prepare for class, back to the library. And that's just the faculty. A university is the dwelling place of a multitude of people running, breathless, to the next assignment. I suspect that you know that tempo, too.

I remember the day well, it was a Monday. Late that afternoon in my office at the church I was getting ready for our church board meeting in just an hour or so. Our youth pastor Michael Goetz stuck his head in the door. And in a flash we were back in the conversation from our senior leader staff meeting earlier—we were talking vision. I recalled with him the words of the Chicago architect, Daniel Burnham: "Make no small plans, for they do not contain the magic to stir men's souls." "You know what we need, don't you? We need a huge, God-sized vision to drive us into the future." Michael responded, "What we need is a generation of young missionaries to reach the young right here—peer to peer—motivated, mentored, mobilized. We need

God to blow open this place with a Holy Spirit revival—that's what we need!" We knelt and prayed together. Michael left.

A few seconds later there's a knock on my door. "Yo," I call out. Jonathan, a university student, pokes his head in, "Pastor, can we talk?" "Listen, my man, I've got a church board meeting in 20 minutes—and I chair it—so no, this isn't a very good time—but what's up?"

As though I had invited him in, he goes on, "I've been walking around campus and praying and thinking how much we need God to do something major in this place." *Suddenly this conversation feels strangely familiar.* "Sit down," I say.

"Could we call a special Day of Prayer for all the students?" he asks. My weak faith replies: "Look, we're four days away from the end of the year—I think it's too late. But *here's what you can do—find a dozen of your friends and peers to join you in praying, really praying, all through this summer that God will do something supernatural, something way outside the box, this next school year. Then come back here and let's go for it.*" We pray together, and he leaves.

Ten minutes till board now—I sat there by my window, brooding over the voices of the last hour. I decided to go the board and simply share what I had heard. I told the two stories, then scribbled on the white board a line from a book on prayer I've been reading, *"If you will find voice and time to pray, God will find time and voice to answer."* (Prayer, 100) I asked, "What God-sized dream do you think God wants us to be asking Him for, for this new year just a summer away?"

That collective conversation—for me—was a paradigm-shifting moment. Rather than discussing some small, incremental, cosmetic changes for the new year ahead, we were asking, *What God-sized request should we be pleading for?* We concluded with an earnest season of prayer. In my mind the die had been cast. God was up to something out-of-the-ordinary.

The very next week I spent an afternoon in a planning session with our media director, Nick Wolfer, and our campus chaplain, José Bourget. The conversation eventually turned to spiritual life on the campus. José reflected on some of the student interviews he had just finished, looking for new year leadership. "I'm amazed," he commented, "at the moral ambiguity that our students express." So what do you think a revival on this campus would look like? I asked him. "I imagine students gathered in small prayer groups, on the sidewalks, in the hallways, in the cafeteria, the dorm—a spontaneous and public seeking after God." Could it happen here? We prayed together.

So I'm hearing all these voices. And then came the voice of God. The principal of the academy on our campus had asked me to bring a 10-minute worship thought to his students the next morning. That evening I spent an hour and a half working on it. When I finished writing, I knelt by my desk to ask God to give the devotional a special anointing the next morning. No sooner had I begun my prayer than I heard a Voice inside of me that said, "Nice devotional, Dwight, but the wrong one."

I came straight up off my knees, "You've got to be kidding me!" He wasn't. So I sat back down at my desk, pulled out the yellow pad again and began to write. About the voices I'd been hearing the past few weeks, about feeling convicted that God wanted to raise up a new generation of moral leaders on our campus—at both the university and the high school. I woke up the next morning at 4:45 with the academy on my mind. I went down to my study to pray, and I knew in my heart that the Voice was right. This appeal was what needed to happen on that campus this morning.

I went for my morning run and showed up at the chapel at 8:45. Before the kids started coming in, the principal came in and sat beside me, "What shall I pray for you?" he asked. I told him what had happened, about rewriting the devotional, and asked him to pray for the students' decisions.

I admit that it wasn't a very polished 10 minutes but it was from my heart, and I ended with an appeal that they would be willing to be called and shaped by God to become moral leaders on campus. I invited them to join me and Jonathan and Michael and José *in praying all summer long for God to do something supernatural in our hearts and on our campuses in the new school year.* A lot of them stood. Not all, but a lot.

I was feeling a bit embarrassed by having a devotional so unpolished so after greeting a few of the students I decided to slip out of the chapel and head back to my study. But I got only two blocks away when that same Voice spoke again, "What in the world are you doing, Dwight! You're missing the whole point of My sending you there. Go back."

So I turned around, drove back to the campus, and decided to talk with one of the seniors I had seen sitting on the front row. I found him in a study hall, and we went back to the chapel. His openings words, "Pastor, I've been thinking about that call to be a moral leader—and I want to offer my life to God to be just that." We talked and then prayed together. As I walked past the principal's office, the door was open and I stuck my head in. "Dwight, I've been sitting here thinking about this call for moral leaders. I need you to know I'm ready to do whatever it takes to see them raised up." We talked and then prayed together. I then left the building and ran into the academy Bible teacher. "Thanks for the appeal, Dwight. Of course all the kids didn't stand. But as soon as you began that invitation, I watched one of the girls sitting there. I know what she's like; she'll never stand, I thought to myself. But I was amazed—she stood!"

Finally I drove back to my study. But now with even more voices in my mind. And I am overcome with the thought that God truly is up to something. There are too many coincidentals to be coincidental. I sat down at my desk. And I tell you the truth, that Voice, I hear it again. "Looks like you're going to need to change the new pulpit series you've been planning, doesn't it?" I knew the answer. We need to seize the moment. Because it really is time for God to do "a new thing." Too many voices; too clear to be misunderstood.

So that's the story that has brought me—and now us—to this moment. I believe it is not by accident that you are reading this book. But it confronts us with a critical question for this generation: What is this "new thing" God promises to do for His people? And how do we get it?

Fortunately we can know. Through the prophet Isaiah God makes it compellingly clear: "I will do a new thing" (Isaiah

43:19 NKJV). No sooner does He make that promise than He begins to talk about water. "Rivers in the desert ... waters in the wilderness ... " again, "rivers in the desert ... to give drink to My people. ... "

Four times in just two verses God brings up water. What's up with all this water? Why is He so big on water? A few verses later He answers: "I will pour water on those who are thirsty, and floods on the dry ground; I will pour My Spirit on your descendants, and My blessing on your offspring" (Isaiah 44:3). Why, it's the very promise Jesus Himself echoed in His familiar but stunning words: "Let anyone who is thirsty come to me and drink. Whoever believes in me, as the Scripture has said, rivers of living water will flow from within them." John then clarifies, "By this he meant the Spirit, whom those who believed in Him were later to receive" (John 7:37, 38 NIV).

There it is—a Holy Spirit baptism for a new generation. And the result? Living water flowing from within them to their world.

I remind you that in the arid Middle East where Isaiah and Jesus lived, water is the most precious commodity, the greatest blessing of all. For wherever there is water in the desert there is life. When you fly out West over the brown wilderness plains of the U.S. what stands out with such stunning contrast are those patches of irrigated farmland—dark rich green circles against the barren dry desert. When the Holy Spirit fills you, Jesus declares unequivocally, "You will not be able to contain the life-giving water that will flow from you to the world around you, bringing life, green, verdant life wherever you go." Wow! What a promise! What a glorious "new thing" He offers.

Heaven has no gift greater than the water of the Spirit of Christ. That gift brings all others. Listen to the words of one who understood that so well: "This promised blessing, claimed by faith, brings all other blessings in its train." And don't miss this: " ... He is ready to supply every soul according to the capacity to receive." (*Desire of Ages*, 672)

The key word for the reception of God's gift of the Spirit in both Isaiah and John is the word "thirsty." How thirsty are you for the water of the Spirit of Christ? Remember Jonathan, the student who came to my office? I bumped into him a few days later on campus. He said, "Pastor, let me show you something." He pulled out his smart phone and opened up a page where he had written the names of eight students who had covenanted to pray intensely with him all summer long for the outpouring of the Holy Spirit on our campus. Only four to go. Jonathan was thirsty.

My friend Ron Clouzet, in his powerful book on the outpouring of the Holy Spirit, renders this disturbing diagnosis—is it true about me, too?

> Admittedly, in vast areas of the western world, we are a church in decline. Our preoccupation for the things of the world, and our searing blindness to our true condition, have made of us—who have talent, resources, and much history in Jesus—a puny spiritual people. We really are terminally ill, but little do we know it. We've been medicating for so long that we don't know what health is like any more. … What we desperately need is a double dose of spiritual aid—a revelation of the character of Christ and a thorough baptism of the Spirit. (*Adventism's Greatest Need*, 184)

Ron is right, isn't he? Have we been self-medicating so long, we're not even thirsty anymore? To us then God comes with His quiet promise: "Behold I will do a new thing—I will pour My Spirit on those who are thirsty." To you first, then to your friends, then to your community, then to your world.

And so I invite you to put your finger on Isaiah 43:19 or across the page on Isaiah 44:3. Pray the prayer, "O God, please do a 'new thing,' in our midst. And start with me. Right now. Raise up a new generation of students and parents and churches and pastors and leaders who will come, thirsty every day, and say, 'Here I am, Lord. I'm ready to have You do Your work in me and I'm ready to go wherever You ask and do whatever You say.' "

After all, it is time, high time, that you and I listen to that Voice, isn't it?

CHAPTER 3

THE CIRCLE MAKER

Dwight K. Nelson

A drought is like being thirsty, only on steroids. The whole land is thirsty. The lakes are thirsty. The streams are thirsty. The trees are thirsty. The cows are thirsty. The birds are thirsty. All across the stark, un-fruited plain everything that lives is dying. Of thirst. If you've ever been thirsty, really thirsty, you will recognize a drought as thirst writ large.

As Honi, a Jewish sage, approaches the marketplace, nearly barren now from the drought, some in the crowd recognize him. Driven by the desperation of many months of cloudless skies and burning sun, one of them calls to him, "Honi, pray that rain may fall." Quickly, other voices, weary with their own vacant prayers, call out the same plea.

Honi lifts his eyes to heaven and cries to the Lord God for rain. The crowd scarcely breathes, only waits. Nothing. There is nothing. No rain, no thunder. Not even a cloud. "He prayed, but the rain did not fall," record the Mishna and Jewish historian, Josephus.

So Honi does what would be told and retold for generations to come. He takes his staff, thrusts its wooden tip into the dry ground, and draws a large circle around himself.

Then, before the wondering eyes of the throng, Honi lifts his head to the brassy heavens and cries out, *"O Lord of the world, your children have turned their faces to me … I swear by your great name that I will not stir from here until you have pity on your children."*

The Mishna reads, "Rain began falling drop by drop …

until the Israelites had to go up to the Temple Mount because of the rain." And thus is born the 1st century BC legend of Honi, the circle maker.

You and I would agree that there are times in life when our very souls are compelled to draw a circle and step into it. "O, God," we hear ourselves say, "I am not leaving this circle until You answer my prayers." I have heard parents pray with that desperation over a wayward child. I have heard husbands and wives cry over a broken marriage with such intensity … "O, God—I am not leaving this circle … " All of us have felt compelled to step into such a circle with God. It may be over your career. Or your health. Your finances. Your sanity. Or a dream you refuse to relinquish, pleading with God for its fulfillment. "O, God—I am not leaving this circle until You answer my prayers."

Mark Batterson, in his stirring book *The Circle Maker*, describes such praying:

> Desperate times call for desperate measures, and there is no more desperate act than praying hard. There comes a moment when you need to throw caution to the wind and draw a circle in the sand. There comes a moment when you need to defy protocol, drop to your knees, and pray for the impossible. There comes a moment when you need to muster every ounce of faith you have and call down rain from heaven. (84)

Question: Is such a prayer presumptuous … naïve … mistaken … misguided? Apparently the Holy Spirit thinks not. For was it not the guilt-ridden Jacob who clung to the arms and sweaty torso of his Midnight Assailant at Brook Jabbok and declared, "I will not let You go unless you bless me!"? … I am not leaving this circle until You answer my prayer.

"Yes, but maybe that's just an Old Testament aside to soothe our midnight anxieties … " Really? Jesus didn't think so—for He told His own story that unmistakably drives home this solitary point. Listen: "Then Jesus told His disciples a parable to show them that they should always pray and not give up." (Luke 18:1) "O, God, I will not let you go unless you bless me." O God, I am not leaving this circle until you answer my prayer.

It has been my privilege to serve as pastor of the campus church at Andrews University in Michigan for more than three decades. Each year, as the students begin to arrive—from all over the world—it is a time of uneasy excitement for those of us who welcome them. These bright young adults will have their lives changed during the nine months they will spend on campus.

They will leave here different—significantly different—than when they arrived. They'll go back—to Boston and Bangkok, to San Francisco and Sao Paulo—and change their worlds.

What must happen here to help make it possible for God to fulfill His destiny-dreams for this generation of the young? In other words, what should we be pounding the gates of heaven for? What kinds of circles should we draw? We pray every school year that God will make His presence felt on campus and lead our students and staff, first to a growing journey with Jesus, and then that He will guide them in their appointed mission. But recently we had a sense that God wanted to do something totally out of the ordinary, that He wanted to do "a new thing."

We made that discovery on the strength of His promise in Isaiah 43:19-20 that He will "do a new thing." Through the ancient prophet God begins talking about water—springs in the desert and rivers in the wilderness, water to drink. Four times in two verses He refers to water. And a few verses later He reveals what this promise of water is all about.

Listen: "I will pour water on those who are thirsty, and floods on the dry ground; I will pour My Spirit on your descendants, and My blessing on your offspring." (Isa. 44:3)

There it was—a two-line divine promise to "do a new thing" for His people: "I will do a new thing—I will pour water on those who are thirsty, and My Spirit on your descendants."

The promise is there. But how do we access it? I have prayed more than once and then wondered if I would even know it if God were to answer. Cursory prayers. Drive-thru prayers. Prayers I know I should pray. I've prayed for things as passionately as children with their Sunday newspaper Toys-R-Us circular—"Look, Daddy—this is the toy I've been wanting my whole life!"—until, of course, next week, and the next toy ad! But God honors tenacity.

David A. Redding, in his masterful treatment of Jesus' parables, *The Parables He Told*, cuts to the chase with the widow and the judge parable:

> This story shouts that prayer isn't any good unless it is persistent. God won't give us what we want the first time we ask for it—what Robert Collyer called: 'The determination of heaven not to hear what we are not determined that heaven shall hear.' (39)

Jesus wanted us to know that. Remember the fascinating story He told for the express purpose of imprinting on our hearts the essential truth that we "should always pray and not give up." It's recorded in Luke 18 and we call it "The Parable of the Persistent Widow."

But is claiming this "new thing," for which we've prayed a thousand times, nothing more than the tacit admission we have previously failed those times in our prayer mission? No. It is rather the recognition before God that while we are humbled and grateful for the uncounted blessings of heaven, we still must confess that we have been unable to break out of the spiritual status quo that we repeat year after year. Surely our hearts acknowledge that there must be more that God has promised than we have experienced thus far. There is, and as Pastor Batterson would remind us, God honors bold prayers because bold prayers honor God.

Powerful insight: "There is no danger that the Lord will neglect the prayers of His people. The danger is that they will become discouraged, and fail to persevere in prayer." (*Christ's Object Lessons*, 175)

So, He promises: "I will do a new thing—I will pour water on those who are thirsty, and My Spirit on your descendants." I asked myself, "What would such a "new thing" look like? Or maybe we should be asking, "What *will* such a new thing look like?" It will be different where you serve, but attempting to dream God's dream with Him is a spiritually energizing exercise.

Let me share with you a story that I believe glimpses into the realm of God's explosive possibilities. My friend, Ron Clouzet, cites it in his exhilarating book, *Adventism's Greatest Need*. With his permission I want to present it just as he has written it. I warn you, this will make you thirsty for the floods God has promised.

> In the days right before the collapse of communism, life was tough for Romanian Adventists. Lack of available goods, rampant political corruption, and poverty dominated people's lives. But my friend Pavel was a rich man. He'd been faithful to God in everything he knew, risking education, advancement, and opportunities, to honor the Sabbath and other Bible teachings.
>
> God rewarded such faithfulness by placing him as the owner of a sewing business which made serious money. He was taking in more than half a million dollars a year and was poised, in association with a German company, to quadruple that income. As [Pavel and his wife] were asking God whether or not to take that step in business, the [Adventist Church in Romania] called him to be a full-time pastor. They had no clue what he was making. A pastor's salary was $250 a month, a tenth of 1 percent of his potential income.
>
> He and Dana, his wife, decided to surrender all to Jesus. They sold their nice home and cars and gave away practically everything they owned. They bought an old Russian jalopy, a little box on wheels, so as not to make their members envious. But they found their four-church district to be a complete mess …
>
> [Pavel] decided to practice the fundamentals. He encouraged families to gather together for seasons of prayer … Within two years the membership doubled. As they reached out to friends and neighbors, they added a new congregation and two new companies [of

believers] to the district. This kind of progress doesn't go unnoticed by the enemy of souls, and he prepared a counterattack to strike just two weeks before the start of Pavel's next evangelistic series of meetings.

As he drove outside of Otelu Poru one day, a teen decided to cross the highway without looking in his direction. The car struck the boy's hip and leg and sent him flying straight up in the air, only for him to land right in front of Pavel, too late to avoid his hitting the boy again, this time in the head and shoulders. The teenager's body was a crumpled mess, with blood running out of his ears, nose, mouth, and eyes. He was rushed to the hospital. His brain hemorrhaged profusely; his spine was broken in two places; one of his lungs was punctured; and he had a broken hip, arm, and leg. A team of physicians did their best to save him but without success. After he died, they covered him with a sheet, and each one filed out of the emergency room, leaving the boy, Mene Mene, to be taken to the morgue later.

Poor Mene Mene had been a 19-year-old, well known in town. Suffering from motor coordination deficiencies, he couldn't control his arms or legs well and had come close to being killed crossing the street on more than one occasion. People had given him the nickname to ridicule his stuttering problem. Now, the Adventist pastor had killed one of the best-recognized characters in town. And Pavel was devastated by the loss of that innocent young life and the damage to God's cause, at a time when the Spirit was blessing them so much.

Pavel remained next to Mene Mene's bed, praying for him.

"God, what are the people of Otelu Poru going to say when they hear that I killed a young man just beginning his life? They know I'm a pastor. What will they think? If need be, I am willing to exchange my life for his. I know You are able to bring him back to life if you choose. I'm asking You—please bring him back. Please, God—please."

One of the doctors caught him praying and told him to go home. He assured Pavel that the boy was very dead and that it was too late to pray for him now.

"Just face it—it's over," he said.

But Pavel believed in a bigger God than those communist doctors had ever dreamed of. Back home, he and his wife spent the entire night pleading before God, that if there was any way to restore the young man's life for God's honor and glory, to please do it. And they accepted God's will, whichever way it went.

In the morning, Pavel returned to the hospital to meet with the family but instead found a commotion around Mene Mene, who was now sitting up in bed, eating! He was alive! A host of medical professionals crowded into the room, bewildered, comparing x-rays from that morning with the ones taken the day before. To the inexplicable amazement of everyone, the new x-rays showed absolutely no damage whatsoever to the brain, spine, hip, or lungs. The young man had only a broken arm and leg. In addition, his speech was perfect for the first time in his life. The stutter was gone. And when the teen was discharged, they saw that he had full control of his arms and legs. Another miracle.

You can imagine the news in town. And when the evangelistic meetings began, the whole area turned out for them, packing the church, with many staying for questions after each presentation. The result? The church doubled its membership again.

What will the flood look like here? Different perhaps than Romania. Different where you serve. But as God and I have had this discussion, here is some of the process I think He has helped me to envision. Here are some things that could … that *will* happen.

   i.   Jesus' gift of conversion and reconversion sweeps through the campus.

  ii.   As He is lifted up, a conviction of sin, accompanied

by confession, repentance and a public embrace of the Savior begin to spread.

iii. Walls that have grown up between us—professionally, racially, personally, generationally—are crumbled by the Holy Spirit's "new thing."

iv. People suddenly without timidity and fear begin talking and testifying to what they are experiencing in Christ.

v. Testimonies break forth in dorms, classes, chapels, worships.

vi. Spontaneous prayer breaks out—people huddled together—from the administration building to plant services.

vii. Large numbers of students and faculty join together in these impromptu but multiplying experiences.

viii. The administration responds in support.

ix. The church is opened for informal gatherings—small and large—of worshipers, pray-ers and penitents— early in the morning/late at night.

x. Racial divisions become the concern and public talk of the students—and a move to tear down any racial walls that exist on our campus spreads from the students to the faculty and administration.

xi. A new burden for reaching the lost with the good news of Christ possesses many hearts.

xii. Students organize witness groups that go to campuses near and far to share Jesus.

xiii. A new movement for student missions takes root and begins to spread across campus—hundreds of students volunteer as short-term missionaries.

xiv. Letters and Emails circulate, sent to friends and family in 100+ nations, sharing the testimony of God's "new thing" here on campus.

xv.   Soon teams of students and faculty are traveling internationally to meet with other youth groups/ campuses to share their experience and facilitate "a new thing" around the world.

xvi. And the "Legacy of Leadership" phrase chiseled in bronze on the John Nevins Andrews statue in front of this church is ignited with new meaning, now capturing God's desire to take from here strategic spiritual leadership to both the world church and the world.

Could it happen? Give me one reason why not?

Then like the persistent, persevering, prevailing widow, will you join me as we draw a circle and step inside it and declare to the God of heaven that we will stay in this circle and pray and pray and pray until He sends His promised rain?

CHAPTER 4

IT PAYS TO PRAY

Ruthie Jacobsen

Shawna comes from the snowy town of Steamboat Springs, Colorado. She's a vibrant young adult and a new Christian. After becoming a believer she soon discovered that there were only two other single adults in her entire church family. This troubled her and she began praying earnestly about it. "Surely," she reasoned, "if faith in Christ appealed to me then it will appeal to other young adults like me."

She began to pray that God would somehow put her in touch with people who might be willing to attend church with her. As she prayed, she invited friends, relatives, neighbors, co-workers, even strangers. Two years later there were more than fifty.

As Shawna learned to pray it moved her to take on bigger and bigger projects—sometimes expensive ones—and each time God provided. Each time He answers she is amazed, though not surprised, because she has learned to expect Him to answer as He promised, and she banks on His promises.

God placed two passions on her heart—starting schools in Africa and producing Christian documentary films, and He keeps giving her opportunities to do both. Funding? He just keeps providing. She may find an envelope in her mailbox, on her desk, in her car. And He also keeps sending people to help her.

Not long ago, she had a painful tooth but hadn't yet chosen a dentist in the city where she was living. She prayed for guidance, then went to look in the Yellow Pages thinking she might find one whose office was nearby. She did, but she was understandably nervous about how she would pay him, especially when he told her he'd have to do a root canal. As was her custom, she took that to God, too.

During the exam, as the dentist was poking around in her mouth, he asked her about what she was doing. She told him that she loved working with children especially and had recently established some schools in Africa.

"Where in Africa?" the dentist wanted to know. "Uganda," she answered as best she could with his hands in her mouth. When she said Uganda, his face lit up. "Where in Uganda?" When she told him, he said, "Really? That's amazing! That's the very region where I grew up; my parents were missionaries." They exchanged memories about a part of the world that was precious to both of them and he was impressed with the scope of her projects.

A few days after her final appointment she received her statement for several hundred dollars in the mail. It was marked, Paid in Full!

Think of God's management of that situation. The right dentist had an office near where she lived—doubtless the only dentist for miles who had ever lived in Uganda, and in the very region where she had worked. She had found his name in the Yellow Pages, remember. Not only that, she was led to a dentist who had a heart to give when he met a young Christian who was giving of herself. A friend tells me that the Hebrew people had no word for "coincidence." They had seen God at work in enough situations, in enough places, they knew that when a supernatural event happened it was because God had showed up.

Moses learned to pray, and it not only changed his life, but it changed history. God does that when we pray, you know. Make no mistake—He would like to do that through you, too. Can you imagine the hallelujah party on the other side of the Red Sea? The Bible says there was a glorious festival of worship; they sang to the Lord, they danced before Him with instruments. There was no way they could contain the joy of what they had just seen. Trust in God creates that kind of journey. God loves it when we rejoice over the victories He provides.

God told Moses that His name is I AM. In Hebrew, Jehovah, or more accurately, Yahweh, is a powerful name for God, and has potent meaning. In the language of the Old Testament it means, He Who Will Make Things Happen. He proved that in Egypt. He demonstrated it again at the Red Sea, and throughout the entire Scripture record. He is the God who provides, who makes things happen for His people. He is the Lord of our circumstances, the Lord of victory in our struggles, and He still brings His people out of bondage of all kinds. He still listens and intervenes. It pays to pray.

How intimately is God involved in the lives of His children today? He even goes before us to prepare the way. (Isaiah 45)

Let me tell you about my friend, Michael Hasel. Dr. Hasel is a professor in the School of Religion and Director of the Institute of Archeology at Southern Adventist University in Collegedale, Tennessee. I met him in Mississippi a few years ago and was blessed by his story. He loves to look back to an event in his life that brought him to his knees in gratitude and worship.

Michael was a student at Bogenhofen Seminary in Austria. He was one of only a few American students, and he was learning a lot; it was a good experience except for one thing— the weather. The entire autumn that year was endlessly dreary. The days were gray, the sky was overcast—and that was the good weather. That became the norm: rain and fog. Oh, and rain. The students on campus were always hoping for a sunny day; it happened just often enough to keep them hoping. On the campus itself, the dominant building is a classic former castle that dates back to the mid-15th century. Bogenhofen is located in a beautiful rural setting four miles east of the quaint little town of Braunau on the Inn River. Across the river is the German town of Simbach, and some thirty-six miles or so to the southwest lies one of the most beautiful cities in all of Europe—Salzburg. So, blessed to be in a charming place, Michael determined to ignore the weather and rejoice to know that he was where God wanted him to be.

He did, after all, have family nearby. The Hasels had roots in Germany, and he was thankful to have relatives near who would provide a good home-cooked meal now and then.

As Christmas approached Michael received a phone call from his father back in Michigan about a large family reunion being planned in Key Largo, Florida, for the Christmas break. He could picture the sunny beaches, fun with all the cousins, and the whole family together. His father phoned to say that they would like to check on plane tickets, and wanted to know Michael's schedule so they could plan the itinerary.

For some reason, Michael didn't have peace about the whole idea so he asked his dad to let him have some time to think about it. His father assured him that he would call back later that day. Michael put down the phone a little troubled, and went over to the girls' dormitory to pick up his cousin, Bettina. She was a high school student, attending school on the same campus. He had promised to drive her and a friend into Braunau for some shopping. When he greeted her in the dorm, he mentioned his father's phone call. "For some reason," he mused, "I'm just not sure if I should go."

"Have you prayed about it?" his cousin asked. "I'm the theology student and she's a high school student," he thought to himself. But he had to admit she was right, he hadn't prayed about it. So they stopped there in the dormitory and prayed asking God to make it clear. Michael had a sense of peace, but still was not absolutely sure what he should do.

As the girls shopped, he wandered aimlessly—even his favorite sporting goods store held no interest that afternoon. When the girls were ready he took them back to campus. As soon as he arrived he was called to the phone—it was his father. His dad, Dr. Gerhard Hasel, was Dean of the Theological Seminary at Andrews University in Michigan. Michael had been in Europe several months and his father began excitedly telling him about all the plans for the family's Christmas break in Florida. "Your mother is looking forward so much to your homecoming," he told Michael. "We all are."

Michael was quiet for a moment and when he spoke he surprised himself as much as his father. "Dad," he began, "I've decided to stay here over Christmas. I'm going to go and be with my grandfather. I hope you and mother will understand, but this is what I think I should do." His father was quiet on the other end of the line, but in the end didn't try to persuade Michael to change his mind. He could see that he had made his decision, and he respected that.

After all the finals and papers where finished Michael went to spend Christmas break with his cousins and family in Germany. It was a marvelous week, reminiscing and learning family history. On Christmas Eve, as they were seated around the tree about to open their presents, the phone rang. It was Michael's father.

"Son, your mother and I are thanking God that you did not come to Florida this year," his father began. Michael responded somewhat bewildered, "Don't you miss me there?" His dad replied soberly, "No it is not that at all, the fact is I had you booked on Pan Am flight 103 that crashed in Lockerbie, Scotland."

Michael stared at the phone and silently handed it to his uncle seated next to him. The lights of the Christmas tree swirled before him as he contemplated what he had just learned. The plane had taken off from London Heathrow Airport, December 21, 1988, flying to Kennedy Airport in Queens, New York. The crash killed all 243 passengers on board, and the 16 crew members. A large section of the plane crashed into the village of Lockerbie, Scotland, killing an additional eleven on the ground.

A chill went down Michael's spine as he reflected on the news reports they had heard in the car as they had traveled a few days before from Bogenhofen to his family's home in Germany. He had not been aware that Pan Am 103 was the flight on which he had been booked, and he suddenly realized that God had saved his life in an amazing way through answered prayer. God had a work for him to do, and only God knew that Pan Am 103 would go down that day in Lockerbie.

Maybe one of the most important things we are called to do as Christians is to remind those around us that God is good. He is faithful and that's why *it pays to pray.*

Rodney Griffin, well-known fifteen-time winner of Southern Gospel Songwriter of the Year award, had been praying for his father-in-law, Reggie, daily for fourteen years. At times it seemed hopeless because Reggie was antagonistic about anything that had to do with God. He hadn't even attended the wedding when Rodney had married his daughter because he refused to step inside a church. But Rodney, his wife Regina, and her mother would not give up. Finally, God responded to their prayers. Let me tell you the story.

Reggie was unexpectedly hospitalized with a serious heart condition and the doctors had determined that he needed surgery. The night before the surgery the family gathered around his bed, all of them aware this could be their last time together. They knew better than to pray *with* him, but they prayed *for* him. About 9:00 pm they left.

That night the Lord seemed to speak directly to Reggie's heart telling him not to be afraid, that God wanted to be his friend. Through the long night hours Reggie struggled with his estrangement from a God who loved him, his own unworthiness, and whether he could really find forgiveness. Before morning Reggie made his peace with God and surrendered. The next day the surgery was successful. Rodney loves to show a picture of Reggie's baptism, and the big smile on this man's face who had been running from God for so long.

But here's another amazing part of this story. *Two weeks before Reggie's conversion,* God gave Rodney this song—about his father-in-law. Of course, nothing had happened yet; Rodney wrote the song by faith:

It Pays to Pray
Hand and hand at the altar, with tears of celebration,
We'd never seen them smile like this before!
She'd spent her life 'a-prayin,' on bended knee 'a-stayin,'
And this morning he surrendered to the Lord.
There's a message in their story, only God can get the glory,
When a child of His keeps knocking at the door.

It pays to pray. It pays to call upon His name.

It pays to pray, to see a miracle displayed.
You'll forget the word impossible when you seek the Savior's face,
You'll know He'll make a way—it pays to pray!

You're tempted to quit prayin,' you feel He's never listenin',
The time has come and you must make a choice.
Do you stop believin' - forget what you've been seekin',
Or do you resolve that Jesus hears your voice?
He will hush the angels' praises, just to hear what you are sayin'
And at any moment now you will rejoice.

Prayer is just as big as God is, Prayer is just as strong as God is strong.
Prayer can reach as far as God can reach.
Don't ever give up, just pray.

Rodney Griffin

Dr. Lloyd Ogilvie, former Chaplain of the United States Senate, once said:

> I have known Christ for over sixty years, and in all those years I have never faced a struggle in which Christ and His promises were not the answer. My problem has not been trusting Him with a specific struggle and finding Him inadequate or unresponsive, but rather not trusting Him soon enough. And in all my years of listening to people and their problems, there has never been a need, a sin, a broken relationship that Christ couldn't heal and solve.

He is willing and He is Sovereign. He wants to show you and me—every day—that it pays to pray.

CHAPTER 5

SECOND DEGREE FAITH

Fredrick A. Russell

My wife and children and I live in Atlanta, and recently I was flying home from Los Angeles after a ministry event out there. I caught the red-eye overnight flight from L.A. to Washington, Dulles, and then back down to Atlanta.

When I got on the plane I was really exhausted, but the Lord smiled on me and I got the exit row and there was no one in the center seat, only a young Caucasian lady in the window seat. I noticed that she was busy writing something, and I thought, "Let her write, God. I'm really tired. I don't feel like talking, I don't feel like ministering. Lord, please just let me sleep the night away from Los Angeles to Washington."

Before the plane left the ground I was asleep, and the next thing I remember we were touching down at Washington, Dulles. As I was gathering up my bags, for the first time I paid attention to the young lady beside me. She had a book in her hand titled, *The Circle Maker*, by Mark Batterson. I recognized the cover and I said to her, "I have that book. I've read a bit of it." She turned to me … and it's a long time since I've seen the glow of Jesus on a person's face like she displayed that day, you just saw Jesus all over her. What she had been doing was really enjoying—all night long—a time of worship there by the window—and I had slept.

She began to tell me about the forty days of prayer her church was going through and about how the "Circle Maker" book had blessed her and about what Jesus was doing in her life right now. I couldn't wait to get home and get that book off the shelf.

I want to share with you one of the most insightful sentences I have ever read. Batterson quotes it in his book. Are you ready for this? Here it is; it's from an old preacher's sermon: *"Never put a comma where God puts a period, and never put a period where God puts a comma."*

In John 11 is a familiar and fascinating story. I have seen this text and you have seen it a thousand times. You may have had this happen as I have, but so often when I think I have found the depths of a text, God steps up and says, "Here's one more angle of this thing, Brother Russell, that I want you to see." Just about the time I think I've got all the golden nuggets out of a passage, God comes along and says, "Oh, by the way, here's one more." I want to tell you that my faith has gone to another level because of what Pastor Batterson helped me see in this text.

You will remember that Lazarus got sick. His sisters, Mary and Martha, sent for Jesus to come and heal their brother … it was only two miles from Bethany to Jerusalem where Jesus was staying so it wouldn't be a long trip for Him. They had faith to believe that with Jesus there, their brother could be healed. You know the story … that Jesus delays four days. When He finally gets there, Lazarus is dead. Not just dead; he's real dead, four days dead.

"Lord," Martha says to Jesus, (vs. 21, 22) "If you had been here, my brother would not have died." Now, if you end the story on that statement, it's all over. It says it all. "If you had been here, my brother would not have died." He was dead. Martha and Mary knew it; so did all of the friends who came to their home to mourn with them.

But remember, "You never put a period where God puts a comma."

Now watch this: Martha says, "But, I know that even now, even though he's dead … four days … *even now* … " See, when you say he's dead what more is there to say? What else is there? End of story, right? Not if you remember, "You never put a period where God puts a comma."

Sometimes we perceive a period to be the end of the sentence, but it may well be that God has just inserted a comma.

We may think that God's silence is the end of the story, but it may be just a providential pause. "I know he's dead, but … " she says, and what follows is one of the most remarkable statements in Scripture. At first you think the sentence ends when Martha says "Lord, if You would have been here my brother would not have died … but You weren't … and he did." But Martha knows it's time for a comma and she preaches one of the most faith-inspiring sermons ever—with just two words. *"Even now … "*

Now I want to explain what I call "Second Degree Faith. In this short story there are two statements. First Degree Faith says, "If you had been here, my brother wouldn't have died." That's First Degree Faith, what I call Preventative Faith.

We pray First Degree Faith prayers a lot. We ask God to keep bad things from happening all the time. We pray for a hedge of protection around our children. We ask God to help us get the job. We ask Him to keep us well. We ask Him to help us with our homework. Help me get to work on time. Help me find a mate. That's preventative praying. That is an important kind of praying but there is another whole dimension of faith. And this is the good stuff … hold on.

Listen to this now. Martha believes that God can undo what has already been done. Second Degree Faith is resurrection faith because it refuses to put a period at the end of a disappointment. It's the belief that God can reverse the irreversible. Do you see why I'm excited here? It is the faith that believes that it's not over till God says it's over. Martha says, "Lord," (First Degree Faith) " … if you had been here my brother wouldn't have died." We believe that. But Second Degree faith says, "Although he's dead, I believe you have put a comma at the end of that story and not a period. It's not over till You say it's over."

Let me tell you about a wonderful couple that phoned me last week. I performed their marriage thirteen or fourteen years ago in a beautiful park in Dayton, Ohio. They are an incredible couple and I love them like they were family.

After a couple of years of marriage they decided to have children. They prayed first degree prayers. "God we know that you can give us a child." A year passed by; two years. They kept trying. Three years passed. Finally she got pregnant on the fourth year, but four months into the pregnancy she miscarried and lost the baby. Then it happened again, she got pregnant and lost the baby.

After six years, the doctor said to them, "Look, I hate to tell you this but you two are not going to be able to have children." I decided to help their doctor put a period in their story rather than a comma. What a great pastor ... I'm putting a period but God says, "Russell, I'm talking about a comma here. Don't think you're so wise that you jump in front of Me."

I put a period in the story and I said, "Hey, you can *adopt*. I mean, all is not lost. I have some friends who run an adoption agency—in fact, I'm on their board." But they replied, "Pastor we want to have our own child." I said, "Well, there are lots of kids that need to be placed in loving homes, and you know what the doctor said. You know what the doctor said." Period.

I kept praying for them and I kept saying to them, "Come on, adopt a baby, adopt. Do this thing. Ten years have passed and it's evident you're not going to have your own children."

I should have told them, "But I know that *even now ...* "

A week ago I got a text from them. It said, "Pastor Russell, it wasn't a period after all. It was a comma. We just delivered a six-pound little girl." Ten years.

Here's a take-away from their story. First Degree Faith: God, we believe you can do anything. Oh God, protect our children. God, please take care of this. God, please help Aunt Esther get well. God help us to manage our finances wisely so we can put our child in a Christian school. Good prayers, all.

But Second Degree Faith believes that God can reverse the irreversible, that God can undo what has already been done. Oh God, how did I miss this before? And God, how often have I missed it? I admit it Father, how often have I inserted a period when You were saying, "No son, that's a comma." How many times have *you* inserted a period where God intended a comma? But listen to me: It isn't over till God says it's over.

What would you put a period behind in your life right now?

- I know the credit report is bad. The numbers are low. They tell you that you need a 770 and you got a 370. You are not going to get the house. Period. A comma says, But even now …

- You're never going to get into that school. Not only is your SAT score low; not only is your ACT score low, they won't even let you in under academic probation. Period. A comma says, But even now …

- I know you got the divorce papers and the marriage is over. It can never be resurrected. But Second Degree Faith is a resurrection faith. It's never over until God says it's over because we've learned that we never put a period where God puts a comma. But even now …

- The doctor's report is not encouraging. She says the future looks pretty uncertain right now. Period. But you put a comma because your faith tells you that God can reverse the irreversible. But even now …

When I presented this teaching to my church I gave them opportunity to respond. I invited them to come forward to the altar and say something like this, "Pastor I've got some second degree situations going on in my life right now and I need to trust God to reverse the irreversible, to undo that which is already done. I want to see my faith—my trust in God—rise to a whole new level, and by faith I choose to take hold of this Second Degree Faith right now."

I invite you to make that same deep commitment as you finish this chapter.

Let me make this really personal. When I presented this topic to my church I invited them to come to the altar with their decisions. Wonderful things happen at the altar. The church was singing,

'Tis so sweet to trust in Jesus, just to take Him at His Word.
Just to rest upon His promise, just to know, thus saith the Lord
Jesus, Jesus, how I trust Him, how I've proved Him o'er and o'er.

Jesus, Jesus, precious Jesus, O for faith to trust Him more.

As the folks streamed forward I felt the need to come with them. I asked one of my co-pastors to finish the service. As I knelt at the front of the church that day, pleading with God for a Second Degree Faith I had no idea what He had in store for me. Now I can tell that story. God often asks me to experience the very things I teach, and sometimes He takes me to deep levels so I can understand.

The following week I went to my physician for a routine physical, but when the tests came back I discovered that my PSA level—a lab test that detects the presence of cancer in men— which should have been between three and four, was 11.6.

I went to the Lord with a new Second Degree Faith. I claimed God's promises. I prayed God's Word back to Him. I spent time with God. I pled urgently for Him to take this thing away. I told Him I wanted to go on serving Him ... but whatever His will, I was ready to accept it. I asked God to perform a miracle and take the PSA all the way back down to normal.

I went back to the doctor and had the test re-run. This time the results were normal. Normal! God had reversed the lab results! You could argue that maybe the first exam was a flawed test, but I will tell you we must never allow a supernatural work of God to be explained away with a "yes, but." I believe that God reversed the irreversible and He reminded me that I should never put a period where He has placed a comma.

You may have reached what looks like a period in your life; God may be wanting to say to you, "Don't worry, my child, that's just a comma."

Thank You, Lord.

Chapter 6

No Limits

Ruthie Jacobsen

Norman grew up in a home with an abusive, alcoholic father. His dad often told him and his sister that they were the two biggest mistakes he had ever made. As a child, the predominant feeling that seemed constantly to haunt him was fear—fear primarily of his father's rage and disapproval. His life was miserable as a child and as a teen the fear turned to anger. He couldn't wait for the day when he could leave home. He wasn't sure where he would go, but he knew he would, and as soon as possible.

Norman's grandmother took him to church as often as she was allowed, which wasn't often, and providentially, one of the things that amazed him most was the kindness of the pastor. He determined at a young age to become a minister. Norman wanted to be just like him.

But one day someone at church told him that God was his heavenly *father*, and Norman decided he could not love a God who was like his father. He could never quite put that picture together as a child, so in his teens he stopped going to church. However, he soon discovered that he was living just like his father. He became depressed and began drinking heavily. He would finally acknowledge that he too had become an alcoholic.

Norman worked for the Bank of America and eventually became a bank executive. There at the bank he met an attractive girl, and after only a short time they decided to marry. Predictably, the marriage didn't last long; they were young, and at that time Norman didn't really understand what a loving home could be … he had never seen one. The more disappointments he suffered, the more he drank.

One evening, in his loneliness, he again found a bar, his usual target for solace. Seated not far away he noticed a young woman surrounded by four or five men, all of whom seemed to be having a good time. He learned that the girl's name was Erika, she was from Germany, and her husband had just left her. She never went to bars, she would tell him later, but that night she was "getting revenge." She was mother of two young children and had come to a time in her life when she was feeling very lost. They talked a little that night, and he asked her if he could take her to dinner some time; so it began.

During their date Norman learned that Erika attended the Seventh-day Adventist church, the same church he had attended as a child with his grandmother. The evening was pleasant, about the first time he could remember being with someone he felt he could learn to love and trust. He asked her if he could take her out the following Sunday afternoon. She said she had promised to take the children to the beach, but he was welcome to join them.

They decided they would both bring food for a picnic near the beach. Norman brought pork rinds, a favorite of his. Erika's 5-yr-old son, Jason, would have none of it. "You shouldn't eat anything from a pig," he protested. "The Bible says it's not good for you. Didn't you know that?" The animated lecture went on and on until Erika decided Jason had made his point.

Seven months later Norman asked Erika to marry him and she happily accepted. They began looking about for a minister to perform their wedding service. The first one they approached told them he would be glad to, but that he always insisted on some pre-marital counseling with a couple first. They agreed.

At one of the sessions, the pastor gave them each a compatibility test to see how well they might get along as a family. What the test results showed was alarming. Erika, from Germany, hadn't been in this country very long and there were some major cultural differences between them.

There were other red flags, too, like the difference in their ages, their lack of a spiritual foundation, his alcoholism; huge issues, all. The pastor cautioned them and finally told them he could not perform their wedding. Norman was so stunned it got his attention; he was determined not to repeat his earlier marriage disaster or follow in the footsteps of his father. He and Erika began attending church with the children and he soon found his heavenly Father to be the opposite of his earthly dad. He and Erika worked through their problems, and later were married.

Their new lives together started at Pacific Union College, in Angwin, California, where Norman began his studies in Theology. His early dream of being a pastor started to come into focus, but before very long he discovered that his studies were extremely difficult. It seemed hopeless. He had never really studied the Bible before, didn't even know most of the Bible stories, and now he was competing in classes where everyone apparently understood the entire Bible. He was in over his head.

One of his toughest classes was Biblical Greek, a class taught by Dr. Leslie Hardinge. A couple of weeks into the course he found the courage to ask Dr. Hardinge for an appointment. When he arrived at his teacher's office he was shaking inside, but as the conversation began he found himself comfortable enough with this kind professor to tell his story … his father, his own problems with alcohol, his life-long desire to be a pastor, his failed early marriage, and his new walk with Jesus. But now it seemed that the journey was so tough it was out of reach.

Dr. Hardinge listened, encouraged him, and they prayed together. "My office door is always open," he assured the struggling freshman. My home is open, too, so come anytime and we'll work and pray through his together. God will show you how strong His promises are. He brought you here for a purpose; He can do anything." Norman left the office that day with a new hope. Those words of kindness and understanding lifted him out of his pit.

There's a Christmas song that says, "Angels are everywhere." Norman told me when recalling the story, "You may tell me that Dr. Hardinge was not an angel, he was just a man, and you're right. But at that time I knew God had sent him to show me His love and direction in my life. God used his words to encourage me and bless me."

Today? Today Norman and Erika and their children are a happy family. Norman is senior pastor of a large Seventh-day Adventist church in California. If you ask Norman what made the difference in his life he will tell you, "It's prayer." His grandmother prayed faithfully for him; his professor, Dr. Hardinge, prayed often with him and for him, and also helped him cultivate his own personal prayer life. Erika, too, has become a prayer warrior at his side.

Norman is a favorite speaker for campmeetings, retreats, and prayer conferences. One of his favorite themes is teaching how to experience intimacy with God. What a journey! It's hard today, even for *him* to believe that he was once the hopeless young man with a bottle in his hand, looking for meaning in life.

I love this amazing promise: "There is no limit to the usefulness of one who, by putting self aside, makes room for the working of the Holy Spirit upon his heart, and lives a life wholly consecrated to God." (*Desire of Ages* 250) There is no limit … God wants us to know Him intimately—and then He promises that He will make us, " … strong and able to do bold and daring things for Him." (Daniel 11:32)

E.M. Bounds was a man of prayer and a chaplain for the Confederate Army in the Civil War. Some have said that no one since the time of the apostles has left such a rich legacy of research into living a life of prayer as he. Bounds wrote:

> The possibilities of prayer … lie in the great truth, unlimited in its broadness, fathomless in its depths, exhaustless in its fullness, that God answers every prayer from every true soul who truly prays. God's Word does not say, "Call to Me and you will be trained in the happy art of knowing how to be denied." Or, "Ask, and you will learn sweet patience by getting nothing." Far from it. But God's Word is definite, clear, and positive: "Ask and it shall be given to you."

Remember the troubling incident the nine disciples had at the foot of the Mount of Transfiguration? The story is recorded in Matthew 17. They knew from experience that God's Spirit can liberate people from illness, from demon possession, from fear, from anger, or from any bondage. When Jesus sent the disciples out two by two, it was to set people free. They knew; they had seen it first-hand.

But now nine of them were at the bottom of the mountain, stymied. They had attempted to free a young boy from demon possession and had failed. Scribes were there mocking them for their public humiliation. Though the disciples claimed God's power they didn't see it there that day and the boy's father became more and more desperate. When Jesus asked them what was wrong, none of them answered. Finally, the father spoke up, described the problem, and ended by saying, " … *and they could not.*"

Jesus reprimanded them for their faithlessness and set the boy free. The situation was difficult, but not impossible. With God there are *no* hopeless cases—including yours—but the first place He points us to when we face difficulties is to our prayer life because that is what puts us in touch with the control center of the universe—and with the heart of God.

Have you noticed that usually churches with disunity and conflict have few people at prayer meeting? Often couples with marriage problems will spend more time with counselors and lawyers than in prayer. Frequently our concerns cause sleepless nights. Jesus says, "Please don't do that. Let's you and I talk. I have solutions you won't find anywhere else. I long to share them with you. Come, let's talk." Magnificent invitation.

I remember well when my friend, Peter Neri was called as pastor of the Paradise Adventist Church in Las Vegas, Nevada. I thought to myself, "Can any good thing come out of Las Vegas? Can any good thing happen there?" Peter arrived, fully aware of the difficult field "Sin City" would present. He knew instinctively that this was a place only the Holy Spirit could set free so he and his congregation were no match for the enemy unless God were to provide profuse amounts of supernatural resources.

So they began, Pastor Peter and a group of church leaders, spending every Wednesday in fasting and prayer for their city. Every Wednesday morning they would climb to the top of a mountain overlooking the entire valley and plead with God to pour His Holy Spirit on that place. The members caught a new vision of the power of God to change human hearts, and a new love for the homeless and hopeless. People, uninvited, would walk into church, witness the power of God at work and surrender their hearts to Christ. The church has teamed with another Christian group in the city and built a ministry that reaches into the lives of many of the prostitutes who walk the streets. The transformations began when the pastor and the members got serious and began pleading with God to do in their city what only He can do.

With the disciples and the helpless father in the story above, they said nothing. They had given up. But contrast that with the response of Jesus, "If *you can believe, all things are possible to those who believe.*" The father offered no excuse but pleaded with God to raise his level of faith. Can the level of my faith be preventing others from experiencing God's power and deliverance? Have you set a limit on what you believe God can do in your life? In the lives of those you love? I love it whenever I see my friend Henry Blackaby smile and say, "Can God do that? God can do anything He wants to. Every promise in Him is Yes and Amen if we believe His Word."

I have another question: Is there anything standing between you and what you know God would like to do in your life? Many years ago a man walked into one of the Christian rescue missions in downtown Chicago. The director came out to meet him and the visitor had a question: "I want to be a good witness for Christ, but it just seems like I don't have any power. I think I say the right things but people don't respond. Would you let me tell you what I say and then you can tell me where I'm saying it wrong?"

The director replied, "There must be some sin in your life; that's the only thing that cuts off God's power." "No," the man protested, "I just think I need to refine my gospel presentation." Ignoring his reply, the director continued, "Why don't we just kneel down here and you confess whatever it is." The visitor was irritated now and insisted, "No, that's not it, I think I'm just saying it wrong. I wouldn't even know what to confess."

Discerning the man's real needs, the director said, "I'll tell you what—why don't we kneel down here and you guess about it." Telling the story later, the director said, "Not surprisingly, the man guessed it right the very first time." So I have to ask again, "Is there anything standing between you and what God would like to do in your life?"

I love to hear Andy Andrews tell about an amazing experience in Mexico in 1519. Hernando Cortez, with 500 soldiers, 100 sailors and 16 horses on 11 ships, was on the final leg of a voyage from Cuba to the Yucatan Peninsula in Mexico. Cortez had come to be known as a conqueror and he had planned carefully for this proposed plunder of what was believed to be the world's richest treasure at the time—gold, silver, jewels, artifacts. The treasure had been held by Mexico for more than 600 years and army after army had tried unsuccessfully to take it.

Cortez had rounded up an army with a level of commitment beyond the ordinary. He talked to the men before they set sail from Cuba about the treasure and what their lives would be like, for generations, when they had captured it. He laid out a vision.

Halfway to Mexico Cortez discovered that some of his valiant warriors had turned out to be whiners. They weren't happy with the difficulties of the trip or the uncertainty of the prospects ahead. So when they landed, Cortez didn't rush inland to take the treasure as he had planned. Rather, he stopped his army on the beach. He lined them up and talked to them about the treasure, why they were there, and what this could mean for each of them. It was intended to be a motivational speech of the highest order.

Finally, it was time for the last speech before the charge to the city where the treasure was held. The troops expected to hear something about an escape route if the arrows got too heavy or where to reconvene if their army was routed. Instead, Cortez bellowed, "Burn the boats!" He explained, "If we're going home, we're going in *their* boats." So they burned their boats, and an amazing thing happened: They took the treasure.

Any boats you need to burn? I have learned that when I am honest with that question, God helps me to get it right the very first time.

The Lord is never content to leave us where we are. He took a handful of unlearned, inexperienced disciples and shaped them to become bold, miracle-working apostles. He'll also do that with you and me so that He can do greater and ever greater works through us for His purposes. Remember, "There is no limit ... " *There is no limit.* Let's ask Him to show us right now how to claim all that that means.

CHAPTER 7

"OverDUE"

Dwight K. Nelson

So I get a text message from my friend Gary Burns. Gary is communications director for the Adventist church in the Great Lakes states. Just a short text: one sentence and three words. The three words were lined up vertically under that short sentence. So I later asked him if he had intended to line up the words in that particular order, since—as it turns out—the first letters of those three words spell yet another word. Another word with its own compelling point. Another word that locks these three words in my memory for good.

Here's Gary's short text on my phone:

Three key ingredients to transformational revival—

Desperation

Urgency

Expectancy

That's it. Three key ingredients to the kind of spiritual revival that the church in America (the world over, I suppose) is languishing for. Three words that spell D-U-E. Three words that are past DUE, that are over DUE for us today, are they not?

You say, "But really—what do these three words have to do with this rather stunning promise of God we've been contemplating in this book—'I will do a new thing'?" They have everything to do with it!

"I will do a new thing. . . . I will pour water on those who are thirsty, and floods on the dry ground; I will pour My Spirit on your descendants, and My blessing on your offspring." (Isaiah 43:19/44:3)

Transformational revival—there it is—God's promise for a new generation. The young, the offspring of the church, this third millennial generation—these are the target of God's stirring assurance. "I will do a new thing."

But let's be honest. How really *desperate* are we for God's "new thing" here in our churches, in this generation? How really *urgent* are we for God to do something He has never done before around here? How really *expectant* are we that He is ready to do "a new thing" when we are? Desperation, Urgency, Expectancy—are we coming across that way to Him? When He listens to your prayers and mine, is that what He senses? Desperation, Urgency, Expectancy? Or could it be that D-U-E is long overdue with you and me these days?

This much we can know. There has never been a revival and a supernatural outpouring of God's Spirit and His power without Desperation, Urgency and Expectancy—the three key ingredients to transformational revival.

Which is why there is one more line from Isaiah we must ponder:

> O Jerusalem, I have posted watchmen on your walls; they will pray to the LORD day and night for the fulfillment of his promises. Take no rest, all you who pray. Give the LORD no rest until he makes Jerusalem the object of praise throughout the earth. (Isaiah 62:6-7 NLT)

And who is this "Jerusalem" that God addresses? Of course, this is Zion, the people of God in the Old Testament, the church of God in the New Testament, the "called out ones." And who are these "watchmen" God has posted on the walls of this community of faith? We know them well—they are these people of extraordinary commitment to pray on behalf of the community of faith—intercessors of the first degree—anonymous and often unrecognized—men, women, young adults, teenagers, even children who demonstrate before God a desperation, an urgency, and an expectancy uncommon. But not unrewarded, for here God names them as the spiritual sentinels of His people! You know people like that, and so do I.

But we cannot defer to them our own divine calling to prayer. God addresses us all when He calls to us, "You who make mention of the LORD"—"You who call on the LORD"—"You who are claiming the promise of the LORD to do a 'new thing.'" And what does He call us to do? I love the new *Voice* translation's rendition of this line from Isaiah: "Tirelessly pester God—give Him no rest—until He reestablishes Jerusalem and makes it worthy of praise throughout the whole world." Talk about D-U-E! "Take no rest—give Me no rest—pester Me"—with desperation, with urgency, with expectancy.

Wesley Duewel, in *Mighty Prevailing Prayer*, has written:

> The great need of our world, our nation, and our churches is people who know how to prevail in prayer. Moments of pious wishes blandly expressed to God once or twice a day will bring little change on earth or among the people. Kind thoughts expressed to Him in five or six sentences, after reading a paragraph or two of mildly religious sentiments once a day from some devotional writing, will not bring the kingdom of God to earth or shake the gates of hell and repel the attacks of evil on our culture and our civilization. . . . Prevailing prayer is holy work, fervent labor. (20, 21)

How does God describe such prevailing? "Take no rest, all you who pray. Give the LORD no rest until he makes Jerusalem the object of praise throughout the earth." "Tirelessly pester Me!" Only desperate and urgent times will summon forth this sort of praying. But have we not come to such desperate times? At this critical juncture in earth's history have we not come at last to God's promised season of transformational revival? Is it not time for Desperation, Urgency and Expectancy in our praying and pleading before God for the Holy Spirit?

Listen to how *Christ's Object Lessons* frames this D-U-E appeal of God:

> Plead [D-U-E] for the Holy Spirit. God stands back of every promise He has made. [Isaiah 43:19; 44:3] With your Bible in your hands say, I have done as Thou hast

said. I present Thy promise, 'Ask, and it shall be given you; seek, and ye shall find; knock, and it shall be opened unto you.' ... When with earnestness and intensity [D-U-E] we breathe a prayer in the name of Christ, there is in that very intensity a pledge from God that He is about to answer our prayer 'exceeding abundantly above all that we ask or think.' Ephesians 3:20 (147)

You see, I cannot fake "desperation"—I either am desperate or I am not. You can't fake "urgency" or even "expectancy"—you either are or you aren't. "Plead for the Holy Spirit." Go to the floor, to the mat with God for this one gift of Jesus that brings all other gifts in its wake. Plead with God every day for Him to do "a new thing" in our midst.

Do so, and guess what—there is a bonus promise embedded in God's appeal! "The more earnestly and steadfastly we ask, *the closer* will be our spiritual union with Christ. We shall receive increased blessings because we have increased faith." (*Christ's Object Lessons* 146, emphasis supplied) The more we ask, the closer we come. Isn't that incredible? The more we ask, the closer we come.

And it will come—this rainfall. I believe with all my heart that it will come—this "new thing" from God for our churches, for our schools, for our world.

But we must pray. "A revival need be expected only in answer to prayer." (*Selected Messages* 1:121) And so we must pray. And so one more time I invite you—I earnestly appeal to you— to join me and the others in a daily pleading before God for His "new thing."

Does it make a difference, this banding together in collective prayer? Sir John Polkinghorne, the eminent British physicist and Anglican clergyman, visited Andrews University a few years ago. I had the privilege of interviewing him one Sabbath morning during worship. In response to the question— How does this collective praying experience, as demonstrated so often in the book of Acts, really work?—he replied, "I think of group praying functioning as a laser beam. A single strand of light by itself is diminished in power. But when multiple strands of light are banded together, as in a laser beam, then there is no obstacle that such a focused band of light cannot penetrate!" I like that. The power of group prayer is found in the banding together of intercessors, pray-ers, who join their hearts and voices in a single passionate pleading before God. As Polkinghorne put it, " … there is no obstacle that such a focused band of prayers cannot penetrate."

The more strands of light that are bound into this laser beam, the greater the power unleashed by our praying. Ellen White, a century before this physicist, earnestly concurs with his conclusion:

> We are encouraged to pray for success, with the divine assurance that our prayers will be heard and answered. 'If two of you shall agree on earth as touching anything that they shall ask, it shall be done for them of My Father which is in heaven. For where two or three are gathered together in My name, there am I in the midst of them.' (Matthew 18:19, 20). 'Ask of Me, and I will answer your requests.' *The promise is made on condition that the united prayers of the church are offered, and in answer to these prayers there may be expected a power greater than that which comes in answer to private prayer.* The power given will be proportionate to the unity of the members and their love for God and for one another. (9MR 303, emphasis supplied)

"Pester Me—give Me no rest—until I do a 'new thing' in your midst."

In his book, *Welcome, Holy Spirit,* Garrie Williams tells the story of the great Scottish preacher James A. Stewart and a remarkable revival in a European city before World War II. The meetings began with only seven people on a Friday evening, but in five days had skyrocketed to thousands in an auditorium, with large numbers being converted. Stewart was astounded! One evening before preaching, feeling utterly inadequate for the challenge of proclaiming the gospel to the crowd who had gathered, he went down to the basement to earnestly petition God. While praying in the darkness, he sensed a presence of power, and realizing he was not alone, he switched on the light. In the far corner, on their faces before God, were twelve women. And in an instant the preacher knew from whence came the supernatural outpouring.

Twelve women on their faces before God.

Three keys to transformational revival.

One church in desperate need of God's Spirit.

Like the twelve women, isn't it time for us to plead with Jesus, too? Time? More like overdue.

CHAPTER 8

BREAKTHROUGH PRAYER

Fredrick K. Russell

I want to talk to you about prayers that break through the ceiling and into the very throne room of God. E.M. Bounds, who lived in the period of the American Civil War, is perhaps the most prolific writer on prayer that I have ever read. Listen to his words:

> Prevailing prayer is a mighty move of the soul toward God. It is a stirring of the deeper forces of the soul toward the throne of heavenly grace. It is the ability of the soul to hold on.
>
> Restless desire, restful patience, and strength to hold on are all embraced in prevailing prayer. It is not an incident or a performance but a passion of the soul. It is not something half-needed but of sheer necessity.

Let me show you how this works. There is this Black woman whose story is told in Matthew 15, and she has this absolutely amazing conversation with Jesus. And before I even tell you about this conversation, let me warn you that about halfway through the story you are going to want to say, "Why is she even staying in there with Jesus on this one?"

Matthew 15, verse 21, "Leaving that place ... " Jesus is on this series of venue visits and He arrives at a place in Canaan. Now Canaan was literally on the other side of the tracks. The Jews and the Canaanites did not get along at all. The Canaanites were the Black folk of that day because Canaanites usually had a deeper hue of skin. "And so leaving that place, Jesus withdrew to the region of Tyre and Sidon. A Canaanite woman from the vicinity came to Him ... " and she did what? Verse 22 says that she came *crying out.*

The Bible says she came crying out to Jesus, and she said, "Lord, Son of David ... " In other words, whatever I need to do, Lord, Son of David, I'll do it ... "just have mercy on me." And the question is, why is she needing so much the mercy of God? Here is the reason: This woman had a child who was not just failing in school; who was not just talking back to her at home. This is a woman, a mother, who had a child who was demon-possessed. Can you relate to that?

Imagine you've got this daughter whom you have raised and you suddenly discover that the child is possessed by demons. You have tried everything. That's why when this mother comes to Jesus she doesn't come just offering a simple petition. The Bible sets it up well with the anguish and the emotion of the moment. The Bible says she comes crying out to Jesus. And because her daughter is demon-possessed, she says, "Jesus, Son of David, have mercy on me."

Let me make sure you understand the depth of the pit this mother is in. This is not a simple case of a child gone bad. This child is foaming at the mouth. The child has this look in her eye that is full of evil and mother is at her wit's end. But she has heard about this man, Jesus, and she breathlessly dares to hope that He can help her. Desperate. "My daughter is suffering terribly from demon-possession," she urges.

Here's a big truth I don't want you to miss. There is a pattern here that flows all through the Scripture story. Here it is: God has the habit of responding to those who are desperate.

But this story is different from most. When this desperate mom cries out, "Lord ... have mercy on me ... " the Scripture says that Jesus said absolutely nothing. He didn't say a word. He didn't answer ... He ignored her. And I find myself thinking, "What's going on here? Hold on, Jesus. Come on now. I know You heard this little mother ... this is not the way You generally respond to someone in need." Remember all the crowd is standing around. Here's this Black woman who shows up and her world is coming apart. She pleads, "Have mercy on me, my daughter ... " and the Bible says that Jesus did not answer a word.

So his disciples came to Him and urged Him to send her away. The disciples, God's men ... *their words* are as strange as *His silence*. We might expect them to say, "Jesus, come on, come on, she's standing right here. We've seen her daughter and she's really messed up. Talk to her." But instead they said, "Jesus, send her away—she's a nuisance."

As I explore this story, as I dig around in it, as I walk around it and seek to grasp what is happening here, I find myself saying, "God, what are you doing here? Why would you do this? How much is it going to take to break this woman's spirit? Can You not see her desperation?" But Jesus did not answer a word. And then the disciples pile on, "She's bothering us," they whine.

We're talking about breakthrough prayer here. This mother with a broken heart is not going to be denied. She comes before Him now and falls on her knees. Her plea is simple and passionate: "Lord, help me." You can hear the agony in her voice; you can see the tears coursing down her cheeks ... there have been many.

Verse 3, strangely, Jesus seems to treat her almost with disdain. Can you imagine how those words must have stung, "I was sent only to the lost sheep of Israel."

In other words, Because you're not part of the right family I can't help you.

But this woman has a daughter who is in deep trouble and she will not be dissuaded. Are you inspired as I am by her tenacity? When your child is demon-possessed, you don't walk away easily. When you're in trouble or you've got a son or a daughter in trouble, you just cannot get off your knees. Remember E.M. Bounds' statement about prevailing prayer, breakthrough prayer: It is the ability of the soul to hold on.

A few years ago, maybe twenty years ago, Brenda and I had this tax issue. We had someone doing our taxes who was supposed to be a godly person, but they did our taxes in an ungodly way. In other words, we got money back we didn't deserve—although we didn't realize it at the time. We were happy for it then, but when Brenda looked the taxes over she said, "Freddie, this doesn't look right to me. How did we get this much back when we only made this amount?" I said, "Give and it shall be given to you. Pressed down, shaken together, running over. That's from the Word." She said, I'm sorry, but this just doesn't look right. So we decided not to let this person do our taxes ever again. But the taxes had been filed and we didn't pursue it.

Two years later, we were audited. And the IRS sent us this threatening letter that says this is how much you owe, and with penalties and interest, it came to a total of $17,000.

I'll come back to the story. I want to tell it because if it hasn't happened already, there will come a day in your life when you're going to be so desperate that you need God to come through. You're going to know what it means to prevail with God in prayer.

This woman in Matthew 15 is on her knees before Jesus, pleading for Him to help her. Jesus gives her the strangest answer: "It is not right to take the children's bread and toss it to the dogs." He called her a dog.

Now I would have said, "I don't need this." I might have walked away. I mean, "Hold it, I'm crying out to You, I get on my knees before You, and Your disciples too are saying, 'Send her away.' I come to You for help and You say to me, 'I can't be bothered because of the family you come from. The Jews consider you no better than dogs.'" Jesus was just taking the language of the popular culture; she was used to being called a dog. But when was the last time a person that you respected called you a dog? Are you picking up the story? Most of us would've said, "I quit! I'm out of here!"

But this woman stayed at it. Because when you need something from God, you prevail despite the odds. And remember God honors bold prayers because bold prayers honor God.

Now notice the dialogue: "Yes," she says, "Some consider me no better than a dog and all of that. But even the dogs eat the crumbs that fall from the master's table." Her frantic prayer is, "Some may see me as a dog, but if I only get a crumb blessing, give me crumbs, because my daughter, my daughter is going through hell. This girl is full of demons! Lord, You can help her!"

Verse 28, "Then Jesus answered, "Woman, you've got great faith." In other words, many would have walked away by now. But I'm telling you, when you're desperate, you press your case with God. You don't walk away. You don't give up. He says, "I wanted to see how serious you were, how desperate you were. And My response to you is, you've got great faith!" Jesus was going to answer her prayer all along. But sometimes God needs us to press our case with Him.

Sometimes folks say, "If God doesn't answer my prayer in the first 15 minutes, I'm ready to become an atheist. God didn't come through. I'm mad at God." And God says, "No, no, no ... I'm going to answer, but keep pressing your case. Keep coming. Keep agonizing with Me. The reason is this: The time you spend with Me changes you." God says, "The time you spend interceding doesn't change *Me*; it changes *you*."

The last verse of this story says, "And her daughter was healed from that very hour." Now a question for you: How do you think the story might have ended if, when their conversation started and she didn't immediately get the answer she wanted, she had walked away?

Let me finish the other story: So we get this letter this threatening letter that says we owe $17,000. This is twenty-some years ago; I was barely making $17,000. We didn't have any money. So my wife and I went to our knees and we said, "God, Father, please, we've got to have the money because they're going to take everything, God." And we cried out to Him. We were living in Warrensville Heights, Ohio, a suburb of Cleveland. I'm in my first district as a pastor and I'm maybe in my early 20's. Our prayer is simple, "God, we really need You to help us because we're stuck."

After the letter comes we go to the local branch of the Ameritrust Bank and we fill out a loan application to request a loan for $17,000. When we turn the papers in the loan officer instructs us to call back the next morning. We call back the next day and she says, "Mr. Russell, I'm sorry but we're not going to be able to give you that money." I said, "What do you mean?" She says, "Are you familiar with the terminology debt-to-income ratio?"

So I said, "Ma'am, we've just got to have that money." She said, "I'm sorry, Mr. Russell. We can't loan it to you." I said, "Who's above you at the bank?" She said, "My branch manager." I said, "Would you put him on the phone please." She put him on the phone. I guess I was pretty brash because when you're desperate you do desperate things. All the time we're praying, "God, we have nothing to lose here. We've got to have that money because the IRS is coming."

So the manager comes on the line. I say, "Sir, I need to get this loan from you." He says, "Mr. Russell, I'm looking at your account here and I have to tell you that you really can't afford the loan." I said, "But, sir, I need that $17,000. I've got to pay these taxes." He replies, "I'm sorry. I'm sorry, we can't do a thing." I said, "Who's above you?" True story. He thinks a minute, then he says, "Well, there's our area manager." "Fine, would you mind giving me a call of introduction to him?" "OK," he assures me, "I have no problem with that."

The next day, I call the area manager on the phone. He says, "Mr. Russell, I've got a message here that you would be calling, and let me tell you that I'm not going to waste your time." He says, "It is clear that you cannot afford this loan and we can't loan it to you. I'm really sorry." I said, "Sir, you don't understand. The Internal Revenue Service is coming after my wife and me. We need the money. Who's above you?" True story. He says, "Well, we've got our district manager." I said, "Would you mind giving him a call of introduction for me?" He gave me a call of introduction.

I called the man the next day and I said, "Sir, this is Mr. Russell." He immediately answered, "Mr. Russell, I've been hearing a lot about you."

I said, "Well sir, do you know what's going on here? We've got to have that money." "Mr. Russell, I hear you. I hear what you're saying, but we cannot loan you the money."

I said, "Sir, who's above you? He says, "There is an area

vice president." I said, "Would you mind giving me a call of introduction to him?" I'm like that woman. Call me a dog. Say anything you want, but I need this loan to be approved. So he gave me the number of the area vice president.

I call his office and the administrative assistant comes on. "Mr. Russell, we're aware of you. Mr. Genrep wants you to come in on Wednesday morning. Can you make that?" Oh, praise God! We're over the first hurdle!

Three days later Brenda and I and Andy and Ashley, our very small kids, walk into the bank. We go up to the top floor of this huge bank right downtown, and when the elevator doors open we step out onto carpet so thick we're bouncing as we're walking in. As we head toward his office I said, "Brenda, look poor, or something." We walk into the vice-president's office, corner office, top floor of the bank.

As we walked into the office, the administrative assistant says, "You must be Pastor Russell." I said, "Yes, I am." She says, "Have a seat, Mr. Genrep will be right with you." We sat down for a few minutes, and then her telephone rings. She picks it up. "Yes, sir, Pastor and Mrs. Russell are here." So Ashley and Andy stay with the assistant and Brenda and I walk into the office.

Mr. Genrep gets up from his massive oak desk and welcomes us. He says, "Pastor Russell, right? I'm so glad to meet you. Please have a seat." He continues, "Now I've heard that you have been really pressing our bank to grant this loan. A lot of people know about you around the bank, you know. Now I want you to tell me from the beginning what your story is. I've got your file here but I'm just going to push it to the side and listen."

Well I had financial reports, statements of our family's finances showing our plan to repay the loan, and I walked him through all of it. I told him about the tax situation and how we had been audited. He asked a few questions but mostly he listened.

Finally he says, "Pastor Russell, you know, let me tell you something you'll find interesting. My priest had the same problem." I said, "Oh dear God, where is this going?" Mr. Genrep continues, "Pastor Russell, you need some tax help." Brenda is sitting beside me praying quietly. "So let me see if we can't work this out."

He picks up his phone and says, "John, this is Bob." "Hmm," I'm thinking, John and Bob; maybe this is going to be OK." He continues, "John, I've got one of my best customers here." I nudge Brenda, "I'm his best customer?" "John, I want to bring him down to you." He's vice-president of the bank, and he wants to bring me down to see John? OK, maybe this is going to work.

He takes Brenda and me, Ashley and Andy, and we go down to the next floor. We walk into this corporate boardroom, there's mahogany wood all over the place, and John says, "Bob, I'd like you to help Pastor and Mrs. Russell. They've got a little trouble here on their taxes." Bob replies, "I'll tell you what, let me get my top tax accountant on it." We weren't even part of the conversation. We were sitting there just praying, "God, please help us."

A few minutes later, in walks this guy named Phil. John says, "Phil, this is the situation. See if you can help Pastor and Mrs. Russell." Bob and John leave the room; Phil sits down and begins to flip through my tax papers. After a few minutes he says, "Well, Pastor Russell, I think we can help you."

I said, "Praise God!" Yes, I did. Phil started smiling. But then it dawned on me. I said, "I don't have any money, Phil, I can't afford you guys." He said, "Don't worry about that, we owe Bob a favor." I'm talking about what kind of prayer? Prevailing prayer. The whole time we were praying because we were desperate.

Two few weeks later, Phil calls me—on the very day the taxes are due. I've got to walk down the street to the IRS office at some point that day and pay that bill. I have no money. I don't know where this is going to go. I walk into his office. Phil sits down; I sit down.

He says, "Pastor Russell, I've got good news. We have been able to check some things out." He says, "You no longer owe $17,000. All you owe is $7,000!"

You know what I said, "Praise God!" He was smiling but I said, "Phil, there's only one problem." He says, "What's that,

Pastor?" "I don't have $7,000."

Phil says, "Let me make a call." He picks up his phone and says, "Bob, this is Phil." (Bob and Phil … dear God, I love this.) He says, "I've got Pastor Russell here and he no longer owes $17,000. He owes $7,000." Bob says, "Great, Phil, glad you were able to help him." Phil continues, "Bob, Pastor Russell doesn't have the $7,000." Bob says "Put him on the phone." "Pastor Russell? I'll tell you what, go downstairs and fill out that loan application again." I said, "Yessir."

So we go back downstairs and reapply for the loan, but this time for $7,000 rather than $17,000. The loan officer takes the papers and begins to key my information into the system. She looks up from her keyboard and says, "Didn't you take out a loan in this bank just a few weeks ago?" I said, "Well, I tried." She says, "Has anything changed with your finances?" I said, "No, Ma'am." "Do you have extra income coming in?" I said, "No, Ma'am." She says, "I'm not sure we can help you." I said, "But Mr. Genrep sent me down here." "Mr. Genrep?" I said, "No, I mean Bob sent me down here." "Bob?" She reached for her phone. "Mr. Genrep? I have Mr. Russell here … Yessir. Yessir. Thank you, sir." She hangs up and turns to me, "Mr. Russell, who can I make this check out to?"

The Lord said, "Freddie, Brenda, don't give up. You keep pressing. You keep prevailing." I didn't have all the language. I just kept saying, "Dear God, we really need Your help here. You've got to come through. God, please help us!"

Keep on prevailing. Keep on asking. Keep on crying out. Keep on saying, "God, help me! Because the longer I stay there the more I'm demonstrating, God, I trust You. I'm not going to turn to anyone else. I'm not going to look to my left or to my right. Your time; Your way, God. I know You're the Rock and I trust You."

Breakthrough prayer is the willingness of the soul to hold on.

CHAPTER 9

THROUGH

Ruthie Jacobsen

"It was the summer of 1984," recalls Joni Eareckson Tada, "and I was catching up with an old friend over lunch. When she asked me about my journey with Jesus, I smiled and replied, 'Wonderful and growing, but I'm convinced there's so much more to know, so much more to enjoy and understand about the Lord, and I've been asking Him to show me how to go deeper.'

"My friend grinned and said, 'Joni, I just happen to have something that may be an answer to your prayer,' and she pulled from her handbag a copy of the little book, *The Hour That Changes the World*, by Dick Eastman."

Joni was skeptical at first because it was such an unpretentious looking little volume. But later as she began to read she realized its insights and directives were just what she was searching for. She made a copy of the page that contains a brief "Prayer Plan," and taped it to the wall where it would be a ready reminder. Each time she began her worship she would dive into some part of the book's strategies, and it unleashed her on the most awe-inspiring prayer adventure of her Christian journey.

From that time on her evening worship time became an altar of praise. As a quadriplegic it is difficult for her to sit in her wheelchair for long periods and she would often resent the early-to-bed routine. But then she began to see her bed as a prayer platform. As she lay there, looking up, 8:30 pm became the most hallowed time of her day. "The hours I spent communing with Jesus launched me into a whole new dimension of joy in the Lord," she will tell you.

Her renewed times of prayer became the hour that changed not only her world, but also the world of her mission at "Joni and Friends," a global media ministry which brings courage and hope to millions. Now, many years later, she still tries to keep a copy or two of what she calls "Dick Eastman's little masterpiece," on her office shelf so when her conversations with a visitor become deeper she has something right there to give.

Joni's is not the only life changed by the truths in Eastman's book. His books on prayer have sold more than two and a half million copies and some fifty printings of *The Hour That Changes the World*, have been distributed in scores of languages.

Many Christians find themselves struggling with questions like, "Pray for an hour? What would I pray for? Ten or fifteen minutes and I've prayed for everybody I know. … " Eastman suggests dividing the hour into five-minute segments and praying a different type of prayer in each of the twelve segments. Praise, Intercession, Forgiveness, Confession, Surrender, Singing (Did you ever sing to the Lord when you pray? David did; God likes it.). The book was written in 1978 and has become a classic personal worship resource.

Dick Eastman is a friend of mine, and he tells me he grew up singing the old hymn, "Draw Me Nearer." One stanza of the song especially spoke to him. You remember the words, "O the pure delight of a single hour that before Thy Throne I spend." He was moved by Christ's appeal to Peter in Matthew 26:40, *"Could you not watch with Me one hour?"* But it wasn't until he was an ordained clergyman that he discovered for himself that this consistent hour in prayer could in fact re-shape every day of his life. Dick loves to quote Matthew Henry's statement from a century ago: "Whenever God is preparing to do something great in the earth, He first sets His people a-praying!"

David Brainerd (1718-1747) said, "Oh, one hour with God infinitely exceeds all the pleasures and delights of this lower world." When I read that I cried out, "Oh God, I want to know that experience for myself."

Study and implementation materials have been developed

based on Eastman's book and classes have proven to be pivotal in churches and communities as groups come together to discover how an hour a day in the presence of God can change them, too. And that leads me to a story I want to tell you. I know it's true; I got it from Dick himself, and he has given me permission to tell it.

One of Dick's instructors, Del Morgan, was invited to conduct a course based on the book for a church group in Arkansas. As the arrangements were being made, the folks in Dick's office reminded the caller that the class could only be successful if each participant had the study manual … everyone who attends is required to have their own copy. "Well, we have 200 signed up for the course," the Arkansas group assured them, so 200 manuals were shipped to be there in time for the class.

On the day the class was to begin, Del flew into Little Rock, rented a car, and drove to the church. As he entered the church office, the young pastor jumped up and greeted him with a big grin. "Guess what," he enthused, "we don't have just 200 signed up for the class starting tonight—we have 350!" He had obviously forgotten that they all needed to have the course manual; this meant that there would be 150 without it. Good news/bad news.

Del, as kindly as he could, reminded the pastor about the requirement that each one have a book, and watched as the young man's face blanched with surprise and embarrassment. "Oh, wow," he said, "what are you going to do?" The teacher felt as helpless as the pastor. "As if there were something I could do!" he thought.

But to the nervous young pastor, he said simply, "I'm going to pray," and he asked to be directed to the sanctuary of the church. The large room was dark, and finding the center aisle Del bowed prostrate on the floor. He had learned that sometimes that's the best position when you are really feeling your helplessness and your desperate need of God, as he did right then.

Dr. Bill McVay, former president of Walla Walla University says that he agrees with Del's premise and has found it to be true himself. I asked Derek Morris about it. "Ruthie," Derek said, "I think it's because when we are flat on our faces before the great God of the universe, it helps us realize how small and weak we really are, and how great is our God." I don't pray in that position often, but when I have I've discovered something very powerful there.

As the prostrate teacher poured out his heart to God, he reminded Him about the total impossibility of getting the books there on time. It was too late to ship them even overnight since the class would begin in just a few hours. He reminded God how essential the manuals were to the personal experience of each student in the course, and pleaded for His help. "I don't know how You could ever do this, Lord, but I'm calling on You as you told me to. You said in Psalm 50:15, 'Call on Me in your times of trouble. I will deliver you and rescue you and you will give Me glory.' I really want this to bring You honor and glory, Lord, but I don't know what to do."

Del's earnest prayer reached the ear of the God of Heaven, and as his heart grew quiet the distinct thought came to his mind, "Get up, and get moving. Go." He felt like Moses must have felt on the shores of the Red Sea when God told him, "Why do you cry to Me? Speak to the people of Israel to go forward."

"But Lord," Del argued, "I have no place to go … where do You want me to go?" God seemed quiet as Del waited for more directions; none came. Finally he thanked the Lord, rose, and walked out to his car. As he drove out of the church parking lot, he reminded the Lord that he didn't know even which way to turn the car. The clear thought came to his mind —"McDONALD'S!" He laughed because he was sure he had misunderstood. "Lord, You have *never* sent me to McDonald's … for anything," he reasoned. Still no answer, so he drove down the street—and soon saw the golden arches. He pulled into the parking lot and walked into the restaurant feeling very strange about this whole venture. He ordered something to drink, and sat down at one of the tables to think and pray.

Lost in thought, he was startled to hear a familiar voice. "Daddy!" He turned to see his daughter. "What are you doing here?" was all he could say. His daughter, a student at a Christian college, and her suitemate, were driving home for Spring break.

"Daddy, what are *you* doing here," she asked? Del explained that he had come for a class beginning that night. "But we are short 150 manuals," he reflected, "and I don't know what to do. "Oh Daddy, come with me. God has just answered your prayer! We had that class on campus a few weeks ago and we had some of the books left over … I don't know how many. The professor who taught the class just held them until I could take them home to you to save the shipping cost. I have them in my car."

As they hurried outside Del moved his car over beside hers, and they transferred the books from her trunk to his. As they moved the books, they counted. You guessed it—exactly 150. No more. No less. The McDonald's parking lot had become a holy place—they were standing in the presence of a miracle.

"But tell me how you happened to come to this McDonald's just now," Del asked. "Oh, Daddy, you'll never believe what we've been through!" she moaned.

"This has been test week and we've been up all hours of the night getting our assignments finished and ready for exams. I was going to get up early this morning so we could get an early start driving home, but I slept through the alarm and didn't wake up till 10:00. My roommate needed to borrow some money, so I gave her what I had, thinking we'd just cash a check on the way home so we'd have money for food and gas.'

"But as my suitemate and I got on the road, we discovered that it's nearly impossible for an out-of-state college student to cash a check. As we watched the gasoline gauge getting dangerously low, we got more and more scared, and our stomachs were as empty as the gas tank. We cried and we prayed, and we didn't know what to do.

"We counted the pitiful contents of our wallets, but we could only come up with $2.31. Finally we saw a big billboard with the golden arches and we decided to at least stop and get some French fries or something and try to figure out what to do. And there you were!"

Sherry hugged her father as she said, "Oh, Daddy, now I

know how I'm going to get home!" They had another little prayer meeting there in the parking lot at McDonald's. Only He could have choreographed these events, and they knew it. "I believe God knew we would need Him when the engineers planned the location for that sign," Del told his daughter. "He must enjoy meeting the needs of His children in ways that are obvious that He had done it, and then He gets the glory."

Of all the gospel songs Bill & Gloria Gaither have written over the last half century, this one may be my favorite. Gloria named it simply, "Through."

> *When I saw what lay before me, "Lord," I said, "what will You do?"*
> *I thought He would just remove it, but He gently led me through.*
> *Without fire there's no refining, without pain, no relief.*
> *Without flood there's no rescue; without testing, no belief.*
> *Through the fire, through the flood, through the water, through the blood.*
> *Through the dry and barren places, through life's dense and maddening mazes,*
> *Through the pain and through the glory, "Through" will always tell the story*
> *Of a God whose power and mercy will not fail to take us through.*
>
> Gloria Gaither

CHAPTER 10

SHAMELESS AUDACITY

Dwight K. Nelson

I remember a familiar sight from my childhood, growing up in Japan. Beggars. Beggars wearing tattered army uniforms with those distinctive olive drab pointy caps you've seen in the movies. They were usually surviving Japanese veterans of that terrible war in the Pacific. World War II, history would call it. Most of the beggars were wounded warriors, missing an arm, a hand, a foot.

It was all you could do to keep from staring. My mother would remind me that it wasn't polite to stare, but you couldn't miss them. They were usually huddled at train stations or busy intersections where throngs would be passing. Three or four or half a dozen, often one with an old accordion playing the mournful minor key music that is common to Japan. A ceramic bowl was usually nearby, for handouts.

They were a common and pitiable sight, these soldier-beggars. Probably not unlike the beggar in our story.

His introduction into the Scripture narrative is simple. "...A blind man, Bartemaeus, was sitting by the roadside, begging." (Mark 10:46) We know that he was not born blind, but he was blind nonetheless. Blindness is a fate that creates limits. He can't read. He can't navigate about the city. He can't travel without aid. He can't work. So blind Bartemaeus begs.

As is often the case, when we are deprived of one sense, our body amazingly compensates us acutely with another. And blind Bartimaeus can hear. It takes him only a few seconds of crowd noise analysis to sift through the excited talk and

68 | *I Go to the Rock*

animated conversations swirling by him now—to realize that the famed Teacher and Healer from the northern town of Nazareth must be passing somewhere nearby. Mark records, "When he heard it was Jesus of Nazareth, he began to shout." (v 47)

Of course he shouted. He wanted to be heard above the din of the crowd. In the language Mark uses it means that he started shouting and wouldn't stop. There is something—when we have a need and we sense the presence of Jesus—there is something that just rises up within us. Even though the bystanders try to quiet him, he will not be silenced. He brought his need with him on this morning and he will not be denied. Jesus was near and this was his chance. "Jesus, Lord, have mercy on me."

You remember the familiar Gaither gospel song, don't you?

Jesus, Jesus, Jesus,
There's just something about that name.
Master, Savior, Jesus,
Like the fragrance after the rain.
Jesus, Jesus, Jesus,
Let all heaven and earth proclaim.
Kings and kingdoms will all pass away
But there's just something about that name.

Gloria Gaither

I hope you know that name. I hope you call it often. "There's just something about that name."

"Jesus, Son of David, have mercy on me." Bartimaeus, the blind beggar, keeps crying out over and over and over. He is a desperate man. This may be the only opportunity he will ever have again to be healed and he will not quit—not now—not with Jesus this close.

"Jesus, Son of David, have mercy on me!" There are some prayers God always answers—this is one of them. Perhaps that's why history tells us that the Bohemian martyr, Jon Hus, bound to the stake, cried these words over and over again as the flames leaped toward him: "Jesus, Son of David, have mercy on me."

Bartimaeus will not quit! Like the persistent widow crying out for justice … you know that story. Like the friend at midnight begging for bread … you know that story. Like Elijah the prophet, pleading for rain … you know that story, too. Those who are determined to have the healing touch of God don't give up, they just don't quit.

Mark 10:49—I love this line: "Jesus stopped and said, 'Call him.'" The crowd, the noise, the bedlam, but Jesus heard. He always hears. Because if His eye is on the sparrow, then His ear is tuned to you. All the midnights into which you have poured your heart—He has heard them all. Your marriage, your job, your finances, your studies, your health, your friends—Jesus has heard every cry you have uttered. Every time you have called His name, He has heard you.

He heard Bartimaeus' first cry. But as God often does—He waits until we recognize our desperation, that without Him we can do nothing, then He commands, "Bring him to Me, bring her to Me." So do not let go. Do not give up. Do not stop reaching toward Him. Do not quit crying out to Him.

And then in verse 51 the story records an unusual bend in the plot. Jesus asks a question we can only describe as strange. "What do you want Me to do for you?" "Hold it, hold it, Jesus— this is *blind* Bartimaeus—what do You think he wants You to do for him? I mean, the man is blind, he can't work, he can't walk about, he can't provide for himself because he's *blind*—what do You think he would want You to do for him?"

But, as Jesus repeatedly did, He now desires that the suppliant—Bartimaeus, you, me—make a specific request as a recognition of our need and an evidence of our faith. And so looking into the face he cannot see, Bartimaeus quietly replies, "Rabbi, I want to see." And in a typical New Testament understatement Mark concludes the story, "Immediately he received his sight."

John Newton, the famous slave-trader-turned-Christian would later write, "I once was lost, but now am found; was blind, but now I see." That is Bartimaeus' story, and if we choose, it can be ours, too. To Jesus' pressing question—"What do you want Me to do for you?"—it is still the right answer; "Lord I want to see." Go ahead and tell Him—He will never be any closer to you than He is right now.

Since this past summer hundreds and hundreds of us here on the campus of Andrews University have been crying out to God to fulfill His promise Isaiah 43:19/44:3 and pour His Holy Spirit on this place and on the people here—on those who walk with Him, on those who don't. God laid that burden on our hearts and He has not removed it.

In fact He has encouraged tenacity with Him through Jesus' story of the man who woke up his neighbor in the middle of the night to borrow three loaves of bread. It seems that a friend has showed up at midnight and the friend is hungry, but there is no food in the house, not even enough for a sandwich. So the man goes to his neighbor.

Here is how Jesus tells the story in Luke 11 (NIV):

> Suppose you have a friend, and you go to him at midnight and say, 'Friend, lend me three loaves of bread; a friend of mine on a journey has come to me, and I have no food to offer him.' And suppose the one inside answers, 'Don't bother me. The door is already locked, and my children and I are in bed. I can't get up and give you anything.' I tell you, even though he will not get up and give you the bread because of friendship, yet because of your shameless audacity he will surely get up and give you as much as you need. (vs 5-8)

Did you catch that? "Shameless audacity." That's the tenacious spirit of prayer Jesus values! "Shameless audacity" for what? Keep reading:

> So I say to you: Ask and it will be given to you; seek and you will find; knock and the door will be opened to you. For everyone who asks receives; the one who seeks finds; and to the one who knocks, the door will be opened. Which of you fathers, if your son asks for a fish, will give him a snake instead? Or if he asks for an egg, will give him a scorpion? If you then, though you are evil, know how to give good gifts to your children, how much more will your Father in heaven give the Holy Spirit to those who ask him! (vs 9-13)

"Shameless audacity," for our prayers, our petitions, our pleadings for the Holy Spirit! "I will do a new thing ... I will pour water on those who are thirsty ... and My Spirit on your descendants." (Isaiah 43:19/44:3) So with *shameless audacity*, ask Me!

Is not this petition, of all petitions, worth our drawing a circle in the sand and declaring to God that we will not leave that circle until He sends the rain? Shameless audacity.

Yes, it can feel a bit foolish—this circle-making tenacity. But I like the way Mark Batterson moves us beyond that feeling:

> Drawing prayer circles often feels foolish. And the bigger the circle you draw the more foolish you'll feel. . . . In order to experience a miracle, you have to take a risk. And one of the most difficult types of risk to take is risking your reputation. . . . If you're unwilling to risk your reputation, you'll never build a boat like Noah or get out of the boat like Peter. You cannot build God's reputation if you aren't willing to risk yours. There comes a moment when you need to make the call or make the move. Circle makers are risk takers.
> (*The Circle Maker* 48)

It is time. I believe it is high time that we take that risk together, that we embrace shameless audacity with this prayer for the Holy Spirit. Will God answer our prayer? Trust me, He is more desperate than we are to see it happen.

The 19th century British revivalist, who came to be known as Gypsy Smith, was born in a tent in the north of London and never attended a day of school. Yet he became a spiritual force in the hand of God in both that nation and ours. Once when he was asked how to start a revival he answered with these profound words:

> Go home. Lock yourself in your room. Kneel down in the middle of the floor, and with a piece of chalk draw a circle around yourself. There, on your knees, pray fervently and brokenly that God would start a revival ... within that chalk circle. (*The Circle Maker* 217)

Shameless audacity, pleading with God to do what only He can do, His "new thing" among us. "Floods on the dry ground, Father. Your Spirit on this generation. O God, let it happen now. Let it begin today. Let it begin with me. Amen."

References

Batterson, Mark. *The Circle Maker.* Grand Rapids: Zondervan, 2011.

Clouzet, Ron E.M. *Adventism's Greatest Need.* Nampa, Idaho: Pacific Press Publishing, 2011

Duewel, Wesley. *Mighty Prevailing Prayer.* Grand Rapids: Zondervan, 1990.

Eastman, Dick. *The Hour That Changes the World.* Minneapolis: Baker Publishing, 1978.

Redding, David A. *The Parables He Told.* Grand Rapids: Revell, 1962.

White, E.G. *Christ's Object Lessons.* Washington, DC: Review and Herald Publishing, 1900.

_____. *The Desire of Ages.* Mountain View, CA: Pacific Press Publishing Association, 1898.

_____. *Selected Messages.* Washington, DC: Review and Herald Publishing, 1958.

Williams, Gary F. *Welcome Holy Spirit.* Hagerstown, MD: Review and Herald Publishing, 1994.

ABOUT THE AUTHORS ...

Ruthie Jacobsen has served as Director of Prayer Ministries for the Seventh-day Adventist Church in North America since 1995. She is also a wife, nurse, mother, grandmother, and great grandmother. For seven years, she hosted a weekly talk show on 3ABN television titled, When God's People Pray. She has conducted prayer conferences across North America and in more than twenty other countries.

She is a member of the U. S. National Prayer Committee and the Denominational Prayer Leaders' Network. Ruthie has written and contributed to scientific and other journals and recently authored her 16th book. Among them, an Amazon Bestseller—God Wants to Hear You Sing!

Dwight K. Nelson, DMin has served as senior pastor of the Pioneer Memorial Church on the campus of Andrews University in Berrien Springs, MI, since 1983. He is also adjunct professor of preaching in its theological seminary.

Dr. Nelson was speaker for the Adventist church's Net '98 evangelistic series, the most far-reaching global satellite campaign ever conducted by the church. Broadcast live in 38 languages, the series reached viewers at more than 7,600 sites in a hundred countries. His books include, Outrageous Grace, The Eleventh Commandment, Creation and Evolution, and his most recent, The Chosen.

He is married to Karen Oswald Nelson and they have two married children, Kirk and Kristin, and one beautiful new granddaughter, Ella.

Fredrick A. "Freddie" Russell is lead pastor of the 4,000-member Berean Seventh-day Adventist Church in Atlanta, GA. While serving as president of Allegheny West Conference of Seventh-day Adventists, Pastor Russell's passion was to see the spiritual strength of its 13,000 members enhanced and their prayer lives enriched. When called to Berean he brought that same focus into his pastoral agenda. He embraces the call of the Lord that, "My house shall be called a house of Prayer." In his personal life and in his leadership, his passion is to keep the main thing, the main thing, and that is prayer. Sabbath attendance at Berean is ostensibly the largest of any non-institutionally-connected SDA church in North America.

He is married to Brenda, the love of his life; they are parents to two "incredible" young adults, a wonderful son-in-law, and an awesome grandson.